Global Strategy for Growth

a Report on North-South Issues

by a Study Group
under the Chairmanship of

Lord McFadzean of Kelvinside

TRADE POLICY RESEARCH CENTRE

THE TRADE POLICY RESEARCH CENTRE in London was established in 1968 to promote independent analysis and public discussion of international economic policy issues. As a non-profit organisation, which is privately sponsored, the institute has been developed to work on an international basis and serves as an entrepreneurial centre for a variety of activities, including the publication of a quarterly journal, *The World Economy*. In general, the Centre provides a focal point for those in business, the universities and public affairs who are interested in the problems of international economic relations—whether commercial, legal, financial, monetary or diplomatic.

The Centre is managed by a Council which represents a wide range of international experience and expertise.

The principal function of the Centre is the sponsorship of research programmes on policy problems of both national and international importance. Conferences, seminars, lectures and dinner meetings are also convened from time to time.

Publications are presented as professionally competent studies worthy of public consideration. The interpretations and conclusions in them are those of their respective authors and do not purport to represent the views of members of the Council, staff and associates of the Centre which, having general terms of reference, does not represent on any particular issue a consensus of opinion.

Particulars of membership of the Centre are given at the end of this publication on the inside back cover.

Special Report No. 1

Global Strategy for Growth

for Growth

a Report on North-South Issues

Lord McFadzean of Kelvinside

Hugh Corbet	Olivier Long
Lydia Dunn	Ian MacGregor
Herbert Giersch	Harald B. Malmgren
Sidney Golt	Tun Tan Siew Sin
Trevor Holdsworth	H. F. van den Hoven
I. M. D. Little	Jean Waelbroeck

TRADE POLICY RESEARCH CENTRE
1 Gough Square
London EC4A 3DE

338.9
G5621

ISSN 0262-141X
ISBN 0 900842 55 5

Printed in the United Kingdom by

Ditchling Press Limited

Hassocks, Sussex

83-1506

First published 1981

Contents

PREFACE   vi

BIOGRAPHICAL NOTES   ix

1 DEBATE ON THE DEVELOPMENT OF POOR
    COUNTRIES   1
  Characteristics of the North-South Dialogue   4
  Demands of the Group of 77   5
  Report of the Brandt Commission   8
  Hamlet without the Prince   10
  Outline of the Report   11

2 ROLES OF PRIVATE ENTERPRISE AND
    GOVERNMENT IN DEVELOPMENT   14
  Development as a Positive-sum Game   14
  Importance of Culture and Attitudes   15
  Role of Private Enterprise   17
  Role of Government   19
  Inward- and Outward-looking Strategies   22
  Foreign Direct Investment   24
  Choice for Public Policy   30

3 ESSENTIALS OF THE INTERNATIONAL ECONOMIC
    ORDER   33
  Institutions of the Order   34
  IMF to Stabilise Payments   35

World Bank for Development		36
GATT Rules of Trade		36
Achievements of the Order		37
Essence of the Order		39
Interests of Small Countries		41
Grievances with the Operation of the		
System of Rules		42
4 THREATS TO THE INTERNATIONAL ECONOMIC		
ORDER		46
Assault of Developed Countries		46
Under-estimation of Market Forces		47
Consequences of Government Intervention		48
Assault of Developing Countries		52
Market Forces and Inequality		52
Demands for a New Order		54
Consequences of Developing-country Demands		55
5 BRANDT REPORT ON THE NEED FOR INCREASED		
OFFICIAL AID		58
Transfers for Development		58
Myths of Western Colonialism		58
The Scope of the Problem		60
Direct Role of Resource Transfers		61
Indirect Effects of Resource Transfers		63
Resource Transfers and the Poor		65
Uses of Resource Transfers		66
Resource Transfers and Recycling		67
Verdict on Transfers of Resources		68
Effects on Developed Countries		69
International Institutions		69
Problems with Developing-country Demands		70
Issues for the International Institutions		74
6 CONCLUSIONS ON A STRATEGY FOR GROWTH		77
Two Distinct Foci of Concern		78
Repair of the International Economic Order		79
Policies of Developed Countries		80

Policies of Developing Countries   82
Transfers of Resources   83
Question of 'Mutual Interests'   84

SELECTED BIBLIOGRAPHY   89

LIST OF THAMES ESSAYS   98

Preface

SINCE it was established in 1968, the Trade Policy Research Centre has taken a close interest in the problems of international trade and investment that have been the subject of inter-governmental negotiations, particularly those which reached the agenda of the Tokyo Round negotiations of 1973-79. As a contribution to the preparations for those negotiations, a study group of the Centre produced in 1972 a report, supported by analytical papers, entitled *Towards an Open World Economy*. Then in 1974 the Centre arranged the publication of a volume of essays, *In Search of a New World Economic Order*, which also recognised the discontent of 'small' countries with the international system of trade and payments; and in the same year another study group produced a memorandum on *The Reform of the International Commercial System*, which dealt with the economic implications of the 1973-74 increases in oil prices.

When, early in 1980, the Independent Commission on International Development Issues, headed by Mr Willy Brandt, published its report, *North-South: a Programme for Survival*, one of the first serious critiques was carried in the June 1980 number of *The World Economy*, the Centre's quarterly journal, in an article by Professor P. D. Henderson entitled 'Survival, Development and the Report of the Brandt Commission'.

A disturbing feature not only of the Brandt Report but also of the discussion of economic development in inter-governmental fora and in the media is the neglect or down-grading of the fundamental role of private enter-prise. Encouraged from several quarters, including the International Chamber of Commerce, some of the Centre's members and a number of industrialists engaged in business in and with developing countries, the Trade Policy Research Centre last year formed another study group to highlight for public discussion and policy forma-tion the role of private enterprise in the process of economic growth and development.

The study group represented a wide range of inter-national experience and expertise. Its members were Mr Hugh Corbet, the Hon. Lydia Dunn, Mr Sidney Golt, Professor Herbert Giersch, Mr Trevor Holdsworth, Professor I. M. D. Little, Professor Olivier Long, Mr Ian MacGregor, the Hon. Harald B. Malmgren, Tun Tan Siew Sin, Mr H. F. van den Hoven, Professor Jean Waelbroeck and myself as chairman. There were two formal meetings, but members also had several informal meetings, while much was done by correspondence. Ambassador Nobuhiko Ushiba, of Japan, although unable to attend the meetings, and not a member of the group, assisted the group in its work. The report of the group is attached. All members of the group are in agreement with the line of argument and conclusions of the report. But, since the study ranged over a broad spectrum of issues, individual members would not necessarily, of course, endorse every detail.

In its deliberations, the study group was assisted by a number of background papers, some of the authors also taking part in the discussions. The papers will be pub-lished, with the report, in a separate hardcover volume next year. The Centre's staff provided administrative support, helped with drafts and documentation and facilitated communications. And the study group is grateful for the assistance of Sir James Murray in finalising its report.

McFADZEAN OF KELVINSIDE
Chairman
Trade Policy Research Centre

London
October 1981

Biographical Notes

Lord McFADZEAN OF KELVINSIDE has been Chairman of Rolls-Royce, based in London, since 1980, having been Chairman of British Airways from 1976 to 1979 and previously a Managing Director, Royal Dutch-Shell Group of Companies, 1964-76, and Chairman, Shell Transport and Trading Company, 1972-76. He is a director of the Beecham Group and Coats Paton. Before joining Shell in 1951 he was with the Colonial Development Corporation in Malaya. Lord McFadzean has been Chairman of the Trade Policy Research Centre since 1971. He was Visiting Professor of Economics at the University of Strathclyde from 1967 to 1976.

HUGH CORBET has been Director of the Trade Policy Research Centre, London, since its inception in 1968 and Managing Editor of *The World Economy*, the Centre's quarterly journal, since 1977. Mr Corbet was previously a specialist writer, covering international economic affairs, on *The Times* in London.

LYDIA DUNN, a director of the John Swire Group, is Managing Director of Swire & Maclaine, Hong Kong. She is also a director of the Hongkong & Shanghai Banking Corporation and other companies. Miss Dunn is a member of the Hong Kong Legislative Council. Among her many activities in Hong Kong, she is a member of the

Textile Advisory Board, a member of the Council of the Chinese University of Hong Kong and Chairman of the Special Committee on Land Production.

HERBERT GIERSCH has been Professor of Economics, and President of the Institut für Weltwirtschaft, at the University of Kiel, in the Federal Republic of Germany, since 1969. He has also been Chairman of the Association of German Economic Research Institutes since 1970. Professor Giersch was a member of the German Council of Economic Advisers from 1964 to 1970. He is the author of *Allgemeine Wirtschaftspolitik* (1960 and 1977) and many other works.

SIDNEY GOLT, Consultant on Trade Policy to the International Chamber of Commerce, Paris, was Deputy Secretary of the Department of Trade and Industry, British Government, 1968-70, having earlier been Adviser on Commercial Policy. Mr Golt was Chairman of the High-level Group on Tariff Preferences, established by the Organisation for Economic Cooperation and Development (OECD), in 1970.

TREVOR HOLDSWORTH has been Chairman of Guest Keen & Nettlefolds, based in London, since 1980, having been Managing Director since 1977 and Deputy Chairman since 1974. Mr Holdsworth is also a director of Thorn-EMI, the Midland Bank and Equity Capital for Industry. He is Chairman of the British Institute of Management and a member of the Council of the Confederation of British Industry.

I. M. D. LITTLE is an Emeritus Fellow of Nuffield College at the University of Oxford where he was Professor of the Economics of Developing Countries from 1971 to 1975. Professor Little has contributed to many areas of economics, first in *A Critique of Welfare Economics* (1950) through to the Little-Mirrlees technique of project analysis and, with M.FG. Scott and Tibor Scitovsky, *Industry and Trade in Some Developing Countries* (1970).

OLIVIER LONG, who was Director-General of the General Agreement on Tariffs and Trade (GATT) from 1968 to 1980, has been a Professor of Economics at the Institut Universitaire de Haute Etudes Internationales, University of Geneva, since 1962. Professor Long was Swiss Ambassador to the United Kingdom in 1967-68 after being Swiss Government Delegate for Commercial Agreements from 1955 to 1966.

IAN MacGREGOR, a Senior Partner of Lazard Frères in New York, is Chairman of the British Steel Corporation, based in London, and Honorary Chairman of AMAX Inc., Greenwich, Connecticut, of which he was Chairman and Chief Executive from 1969 to 1977. Mr MacGregor is a past Chairman of the United States Council of the International Chamber of Commerce (ICC) and, too, a past President of the ICC; and he has also been Chairman of the American Mining Congress.

HARALD B. MALMGREN, President of Malmgren Inc., business and economic consultants, and co-Editor of *The World Economy*, was Deputy Special Representative for Trade Negotiations, Executive Office of the President of the United States, from 1972 to 1975. He was earlier a Senior Fellow at the Overseas Development Council, in Washington, and on leaving the Administration was a Professor of Business Administration at George Washington University.

Tun TAN SIEW SIN, Chairman of Sime Darby Berhad, based in Kuala Lumpur, since 1977, was a senior minister in the Government of Malaya from 1957 to 1963, first as Minister of Commerce and Industry and then as Minister of Finance; and on the formation of Malaysia he continued as Minister of Finance until 1974, broken by a brief period as Minister for Special Operations. Tun Tan is Chairman of the Pacific Bank, Kuala Lumpur, and a director of a number of other companies.

H. F. VAN DEN HOVEN has been Chairman of Unilever NV, based in Rotterdam, since 1975 (and also Vice Chairman since then of Unilever PLC, based in London). Mr van den Hoven joined the Unilever group in 1938 and was Chairman of Van den Bergh en Jurgens BV from 1962 to 1966. He became a director of the main board in 1970. Mr van den Hoven is a member of the Council of the International Chamber of Commerce.

JEAN WAELBROECK is Professor of Economics, and President of the Centre d'Economie Mathématique et d'Econometrie, at the Free University of Brussels in Belgium. He is co-Editor of the *European Economic Review*. Having written extensively in French and English, he is the author, *inter alia*, of *Activity Analysis and General Equilibrium Modelling* (1981).

CHAPTER ONE

Debate on the Development
of Poor Countries

MUCH of the current discussion on the future of the
world economy focusses on 'economic development' and
in particular on what the developed countries should be
doing to help the under-developed.

The idea of the world being divided into developed and
under-developed countries originated immediately after
World War II. It was first projected into prominence by
Point Four of President Truman's Message to the Congress
of the United States in January 1949.[1] This basically
artificial distinction between countries has continued to
be used in public discussion, and in inter-governmental
exchanges, although the nomenclature has changed from
time to time.

The under-developed countries came to be referred to
as 'less developed countries' and then as 'developing
countries'. They have also been referred to as 'the Third
World', as distinct from the Western developed countries
of 'the First World' and the state-socialist countries, or the
Eastern trading area,[2] of 'the Second World'. And more
recently they have been referred to as the 'South', as
distinct from the 'North', which embraces both the
Western developed countries and the Eastern trading
area. At the first session, in 1964, of the United Nations
Conference on Trade and Development (UNCTAD),
which subsequently became a permanent part of the
United Nations organisation, the developing countries

1

began to act in concert as 'the Group of 77' and, although their number has since increased, they are still identified by that term in inter-governmental discussions.

This distinction referred to above is artificial in that countries simply cannot be divided into immutable groups which, by some criteria, can be clearly distinguished from one another. Some of the more prosperous of what are regarded as under-developed countries are better off in material terms than some of the least prosperous of what are regarded as developed countries. Moreover, statistics on national income per capita as a basis of classification obscure the fact that many under-developed countries have rich people, sometimes very rich people, in their populations and, too, that developed countries have poverty problems to varying degrees.[3]

In the late 1960s, the Pearson Commission, admitting the difficulty of defining developing countries, stated that 'few would disagree that countries with per capita incomes of less than $500 per year fall unambiguously in the category of less developed. There is, however, a small number of countries, mainly in Southern Europe, which fall into the intermediate zone between developing and developed countries. In our survey of the past development experience,' the Pearson Commission continued, 'we have included these countries within the developing world; but we are aware that not all of them would be considered less developed countries for the purpose of applying our recommendations.'[4] On the above per-capita income basis, the developing countries at the time of the Pearson Report numbered more than a hundred, accounting for approximately two thirds of mankind.

Whatever per-capita income figure is chosen to separate developed from developing countries, be it $500 or its equivalent today, it does not have universal applicability. The translation of local currencies into American dollars as the common denominator can be very misleading. Per-capita incomes in countries at widely differing stages of development cannot be viewed in terms of American purchasing power or American spending habits. One American dollar buys very little in the way of food or shelter in New York. Converted into its Indonesian equivalent it can purchase much more of these essentials, although less in terms of motor cars, air conditioners and so on—but these last are only bought by a minority in Indonesia.

People's needs vary widely. The relatively cheap wood and attap houses which are a common feature of the South-east Asian landscape are comfortable in the prevailing climate. They would not be acceptable in the bleak winters of the McKenzie River area in Canada. Heating is not a factor in family budgets in the tropics while the requirements for clothing are much less than in the cooler climates of Scandinavia or Oceania.

The main point to be stressed is the wide diversity among the developing countries. Some are sparsely populated, the Gabon having around five people per square mile, while Hong Kong has over 10,000 per square mile. The populations of some are in hundreds of thousands, while those of others, such as India and Indonesia, are among the largest in the world. Thailand has a history of self-government stretching back for centuries, but many have only recently emerged from colonial rule. Jordan is relatively homogeneous, her people having a common language, religion and way of life, whereas Nigeria has many tribes, languages and religions. Political systems vary from Western-style democracies through continuing colonial rule to outright dictatorships. Under their present regime, the Burmese have become an inward-looking people, while the people of Singapore are essentially outward looking. Indonesia and Brazil are relatively well-endowed with natural resources; the South Yemen and Nepal are virtually devoid of them. The oil-exporting countries of the Middle East have high incomes per head, but they are not as industrialised as India.

The differences among the developing countries, like those among the developed, could be elaborated indefinitely. The point is that about all they really have in common is a per-capita income that is below a certain level, arbitrarily determined, depending on the purpose of the exercise, and most of them have joined together to present demands to the developed countries.

All of the above might be stating the obvious. But the resolution of the problems of economic development in areas of the world inhabited by relatively poor people has been greatly hampered by terminology now in common usage and by over-simplifications which, while they may not matter much as long as discussion is on a general plain, make a significant difference when discussion is brought to bear on specific propositions. In discussing proposals entailing special treatment for developing countries, the question soon arises as to which countries qualify and, after that, when do they cease to qualify—when do they 'graduate' to the status of developed countries.[5]

CHARACTERISTICS OF THE NORTH-SOUTH DIALOGUE

The developed countries have tended to see the problem of development in terms of what can be done in practical terms to improve the lot of the poor peoples of the developing countries. The governments of the developing countries have been insisting that the discussion should focus on their demands for a 'new international economic order'. Those demands are set out in the *Charter of Economic Rights and Duties of States* adopted by the General Assembly of the United Nations on 12 December 1974.[6]

In brief, the developing countries argue that they are at a disadvantage under the international economic order established after World War II, the main instruments of which are the General Agreement of Tariffs and Trade (GATT), the International Monetary Fund (IMF) and the International Bank for Reconstruction and Development (World Bank). Over the past two decades they have called for 'massive transfers' of resources, both directly on a government-to-government basis and indirectly through international commodity agreements, and they have advanced many other proposals which in their detail challenge not merely the operation but also the philosophical principles on which the present international economic order was founded.

The developing countries certainly have legitimate grievances with the operation of the international system of trade and payments. But so do a number of developed countries. Grievances differ between countries and do not fall neatly on either side of any line drawn between developed and developing countries. Nevertheless, the debate has been organised as if they do, thereby creating a confrontational situation.

The debate, currently referred to as the North-South dialogue, has been taking place in a variety of intergovernmental institutions, most conspicuously in the fora of the United Nations. Particular aspects of the debate have been raised in the councils of the GATT, the IMF and the World Bank. But on the whole there has been less rhetoric in meetings which deal at a technical level with the problems that actually arise in international trade and payments.

DEMANDS OF THE GROUP OF 77

The 'Group of 77' and the 'South' are labels given meaning not by common economic characteristics but by the determination of these countries to act collectively on the diplomatic stage, coordinating a large measure of their international economic demands. This coordination has proved possible because they all profess to take the same view of the present international structure of economic relations—namely that it is unfair. It is this perception, with its deep historical roots in the colonial past of many of the members of the Group of 77, which has held together the otherwise disparate membership of the 'South' bloc. Moreover, the developing countries think that present international trends are steadily increasing their bargaining powers, provided they act together.[7]

The developing countries want what they call 'structural reform', a blend of political, economic and institutional changes. Some proposals would change the operation of the international system of trade and payments. Such proposals include an 'integrated programme for commodities' to raise and stabilise commodity prices, commitments by developed countries to lower barriers to developing-country exports and to pursue policies to adjust their industrial structures to make room for such exports, changes in the international monetary system which would automatically provide developing countries with an expanding supply of international means of payment, a 'code of conduct' on multinational enterprises which would give the developing countries closer control of foreign investment and, finally, the commitment of industrial countries to targets for progressive industrialisation of developing countries, including the re-deployment of industrial activities and the transfer of technology on generous terms.

These proposals contain analytical weaknesses and a number of inconsistencies.[8] Furthermore, almost all of them would require significant legislative action in the developed countries, either because they imply additional public expenditure or because they entail modifications of private property rights. It might well be difficult to obtain the necessary electoral support for changes of this kind, which imply an extension of government powers.

The second element in the demand for structural reform is institutional. It is to increase the influence of developing countries, first by broadening the jurisdiction of those international organisations in which they have a strong voice and, secondly, by creating new international

6

organisations which will increase their influence in specific areas of international activity. Hence the recent efforts to expand the jurisdiction of the institutions of the United Nations which operate on the principle of 'one country one vote' (for example, the General Assembly and the General Assembly's Committee of the Whole created in 1977) and to establish new institutions, such as the Common Fund (to help finance the integrated programme for commodities), a Deep Seabed Authority (to manage mining beneath international waters), a World Development Fund (to channel aid to developing countries) and a new international trade organisation (incorporating the GATT and UNCTAD).

Constant emphasis on structural reform reflects the shared view of developing countries on the alleged inequity of the international economic order and what they see as its 'illegal' origin (its rules having been devised while most developing countries were still colonies[9]). It enables the Group of 77 to unite in support of international objectives when unity is both necessary for bargaining power and difficult to achieve due to the growing divergencies in the economic performance of individual developing countries. It places emphasis on international rather than domestic impediments to economic growth because it is always more comfortable for governments if they can 'externalise' internal problems.

Although the developing countries hoped to gain by exhibiting solidarity, it is doubtful whether they have. All too often they seem to have held together only to the extent that they could formulate demands of a 'something for nothing' nature. But to be offered 'nothing for something' is no inducement for developed countries to negotiate. Thus although the Group of 77 has been able to stimulate a great deal of diplomatic activity, the 'concessions' made by the developed countries have been less than they look, conceding something on the one hand and taking much of it back with the other, as with the

7

Generalised System of Preferences (GSP) and the Common Fund.

The system of generalised tariff preferences in the markets of developed countries in favour of the manufactured and semi-manufactured exports of developing countries was intended to increase the flow of export earnings to the Third World. But the different schemes implemented under it have been restricted in product and country coverage, hedged by 'safeguard' provisions and limited by tariff quotas, in effect substantially defeating the purpose of preferences which is to provide an *additional* incentive to new investors and new exporters in developing countries.[10] The Common Fund, part of the 'integrated programme for commodities', was intended to finance, through a 'first window', buffer stocks of a series of commodities of export interest to developing countries and, through a 'second window', schemes to promote more effective processing and marketing of commodities in developing countries. The Common Fund has been approved, but action, to date, has fallen far short of what is required to bring it into operation.

REPORT OF THE BRANDT COMMISSION

In early 1980 the report of the Independent Commission on International Development Issues, under the chairmanship of Willy Brandt, was published.[11] The Brandt Commission hoped to find a new approach without worsening the atmosphere of confrontation from which it was felt that the North-South dialogue had suffered in the past. But the report assembled rather than improved on the proposals that had been aired over the last decade or so. It served to focus political attention on the legitimate grievances of developing countries, but, in giving new impetus to some of the proposals for a 'new international economic order', it ignored for all intents and purposes the debate that took place in the 1970s.[12]

The main features of the Brandt Report's approach can be briefly summarised as follows:

(a) There is a belief that the existing international economic order operates in a way that frustrates and impedes the process of development in poor countries.[13]

(b) There is a persistent, if implicit, belief in the efficiency and benevolence of governmental central planning and direction as the engine for economic progress and development.[14]

(c) There is a pervasive mistrust about the working of the market and an assumption that it will, almost automatically, produce 'wrong' results.[15] This seems, in turn, to rest on an assumption that competition is in itself harmful and should be replaced, wherever possible, by regulation. Indeed, there is an implicit distaste for, and distrust of, the structures and processes of private enterprise. Collectives are preferred to individual ventures, resulting in a virtual disregard of the possibility that private enterprise, given the appropriate institutional climate, could be the most efficient generator of economic growth and development.

(d) There is a strong predilection for the establishment of new international institutions and a belief that the establishment of an institution is in itself an automatic contribution to the 'solution' of problems. The creation is recommended of yet another institution so that 'the performance of the various multilateral organisations in the field of international development can be regularly monitored by a high-level advisory body'.[16]

(e) There is much discussion on the distribution of wealth at the expense of analysis of how wealth is created.

All these themes revolve around the central proposition that a necessary requirement for economic development in the Third World is 'massive transfers' of resources from rich countries to poor ones and that such transfers would promote sustained economic development and thus alleviate world poverty. The transfers, it is suggested, can be achieved in two ways.

First, there should be a very substantial increase in the amount of official aid provided on a government-to-government basis or through multilateral development banks; and there should be substantial modifications and relaxations of the rules on the disbursement of funds by the World Bank and the IMF.

Secondly, there should be intervention by governments in the normal process of international trade designed to ensure that the developing countries both obtain a greater share of trade and receive more in payment than they would do in unregulated competition.

'*Hamlet*' WITHOUT THE PRINCE

Discussion of economic development in inter-governmental fora and in the media, in common with the Brandt Report, has paid little attention to the role of private enterprise, even though in almost all developing countries a very high proportion of the gross domestic product is generated by private enterprise—indeed, the proportion is generally higher than in developed countries.[17] The present report, in contributing to the debate, aims to redress the balance. But a coherent discussion of the role of private enterprise has to be set in the context of the principles of economic development in an open world economy.

As the North-South dialogue on the problems of economic development has proceeded a voluminous literature has been generated by the issues posed. As with most complicated problems, solutions have been impeded by over-simplified approaches—of the kind which, as a rule, attract the most support. It is usually the case that

10

deep-seated moral impulses and political attitudes, such as those which the North-South dialogue arouse, can only be reconciled with economic needs—which are in themselves complex—in ways that are not immediately obvious and require serious thought. If there were simple solutions to the problems of poverty they would have been found long ago.

OUTLINE OF THE REPORT

Accordingly, the analysis in this report begins by clarifying, in the next chapter, the process of economic growth and development, before setting out the respective roles of private enterprise and government. Economic development is largely the outcome of domestic policies, which are discussed in the second half of the chapter, but domestic policies can be profoundly affected by how the international economic environment evolves.

Chapter 3 thus turns to the framework of principles and rules for regulating change in a dynamic world economy. The international economic order, as established after World War II, is based on open markets and private enterprise. Reliance on markets, with private initiative bringing about adjustment, is the only way—consistent with the rights of the individual—to ensure peaceful and prosperous coexistence both within a society and between societies. Avoidance of discriminatory policies, within an economy and between economies, is therefore crucial and explains why in the 1940s, following the autarkic and discriminatory policies of the 1930s, the architects of the international economic order set so much store by the principle of non-discrimination.

As orderly conditions, prosperity and a sense of security were restored in the world economy during the 1950s and 1960s, two groups of countries began to entertain hopes that a coordinated approach to their problems might at last be possible. The agricultural exporting countries constituted one group and the developing countries constituted the other. Their grievances with the international economic order are reviewed at the end of Chapter 3. But it is the increase in government intervention in the market process in the 1960s and since, based on an underlying assumption of macro-economic policies that such intervention assists economic growth, that has perhaps done most to weaken the international economic order. It has resulted in conflicts between recently-assumed domestic responsibilities and long-established international obligations. The problem, relating mainly to developed countries, is outlined in Chapter 4 where the impact of developing-country demands on the international economic order is also discussed.

Such is the background to the discussion in Chapter 5 of the Brandt Report's view that substantial transfers of resources to developing countries will significantly alleviate poverty in them and its suggestion thati nstitutional reform could make a difference. The present report, however, agrees with the Brandt Commission that a concerted effort is required to counter protectionist pressures and measures. How that might be broached is discussed in Chapter 6.

NOTES AND REFERENCES

1.The Charter of the United Nations, drawn up in 1945, enjoined its signatories to promote the social progress of all the people of the world, but it did not spell out how this might be done. It was in the early days of the United Nations, however, that the idea of official aid from the West to the rest of the world began to grow. The policy of the United States was launched in effect by Harry S. Truman in his Message to Congress of 20 January 1949. Point Four of that message urged a bold programme to use the fruits of Western economic progress to help the under-developed countries where over one-half of mankind was said to be living in misery.

2.The term 'Eastern trading area' refers, in the parlance of the United Nations, to the state-socialist or centrally-planned economies.

3.The doubtful nature of many of the major statistics which are used rather freely nowadays in international comparisons is recognised. Raymond Firth spent two years in a village in Kelantan before he wrote *The Malay Fisherman and His Peasant Economy* (London: Routledge & Kegan Paul, 1946). Professor Firth was the first to admit that his findings were of limited applicability. Although usually kind and hospitable, most peasants in the

East, as in many other areas, are deeply suspicious; enquiries as to their economic circumstances suggest that it could well be a preliminary to new taxes. They therefore understate the position. Even if convinced that the object is not taxes, they assume in these 'pursey times' that it must be for a government hand-out and so, again, there is an inducement to understate. The concept of ascertaining facts as an end in itself tends to elude them.

4.Commission on International Development, *Partners in Development*, Pearson Report (New York: Praeger, for the World Bank, 1969). The Commission was chaired by Lester Pearson, the former Prime Minister of Canada.

5.For a discussion of the 'graduation' issue, see Isaiah Frank, *The 'Graduation' Issue in Trade Policy Toward LDCs*, World Bank Staff Working Paper No. 334 (Washington: World Bank, 1979).

6.Also see the *Declaration on the Establishment of a New International Economic Order*, and the programme of action, drawn up at the sixth special session of the General Assembly of the United Nations, New York, April-May 1974.

7.Roger D. Hansen, 'North-South Policy: What is the Problem?', *Foreign Affairs*, New York, Summer 1980.

8.Juergen B. Donges, 'The Third World Demand for a New International Economic Order: Governmental Surveillance versus Market Decision-taking in Trade and Investment', *Kyklos*, Basle, Vol. 3, Fasc. 2, 1977.

9.Even so, more than forty countries took part in the deliberations at Bretton Woods on the institutions of the international economic order to be established after World War II, the bulk of them being small countries.

10.A comprehensive critique of the GSP can be found in Tracy Murray, *Trade Preferences for Developing Countries* (London: Macmillan, 1977).

11.Independent Commission on International Development Issues, *North-South: a Programme for Survival* (London and Sydney: Pan Books, 1980), hereafter referred to as the Brandt Report.

12.The issues posed by the proposal for a new international economic order are reviewed in W. M. Corden, *The NIEO: a Cool Look*, Thames Essay No. 21 (London: Trade Policy Research Centre, 1979), which includes an annotated bibliography of the literature on the subject. Also see Herbert Giersch (ed.), *Reshaping the World Economic Order* (Tübingen: J. C. B. Mohr, for the Institut für Weltwirtschaft an der Universität Kiel, 1977); and Mordechai E. Kreinin and J. M. Finger, 'A Critical Survey of the New International Economic Order', *Journal of World Trade Law*, London, November-December 1976.

13.Brandt Report, *op. cit.*, Chs 11 and 13.

14.*Ibid.*, Ch. 8.

15.*Ibid.*, Chs 8 and 12.

16.*Ibid.*, Ch. 16.

17.I. M. D. Little, Tibor Scitovsky and M. FG. Scott, *Industry and Trade in Some Developing Countries: a Comparative Study* (London: Oxford University Press, for the OECD, 1971).

CHAPTER TWO

Roles of Private Enterprise and Government in Development

ECONOMIC development is not 'a zero-sum game' and it is wrong to assume that individuals and countries can only grow at the expense of others.[1] Such an approach postulates that the world's resources are finite and fixed and there is no invention or technological creativity increasing the yield of those resources.[2] It postulates that there is no sense in looking for joint gain because none is possible. But the prosperity of the industrialised countries has not been achieved at the expense of other parts of the world. It is founded on ideas, inventions, adaptations, technological advances—from the loom to synthetic fibre, from the steam engine to atomic power, from the motor car to the jet aeroplane, from the telephone to television via satellite, from the mechanical calculator to the computer, from the circular saw to the numerically-controlled machine tool. These products and countless others had their origins in the inventive and innovative abilities of the peoples concerned.

DEVELOPMENT AS A POSITIVE-SUM GAME

In the process of economic development, the skills and incomes of people grow by specialisation, by the division of labour, by individuals and groups concentrating on what they do best. Specialisation through the division of labour presupposes exchange, a market which can be described as a structure of voluntary cooperative relation-

14

ships; and the opportunities for specialisation grow—as Adam Smith observed—with the size of the market. Benefits arise through the development of an unused potential for greater productivity. In this way economic development can be, and should be, seen as a positive-sum game, both within countries and between countries.

Economics builds a system of thought on a simple set of assumptions. The basic assumptions are that nearly all people, as individuals, recognise the difference between more and less and want to improve their lot. Thus 'as long as three-quarters of the world's population remain poor, it is idle—or the luxury of the idle—to speak of the limits to growth closing in and of growth impulses being exhausted', a recent GATT study has remarked. 'The poverty of the vast majority of the world population indicates not merely the world's need for economic growth but, more directly and importantly, the world's growth potential.'[3]

It is crucial, therefore, that the dynamic concept of an economy is not replaced by a zero-sum mentality, by a philosophy that ignores what the future can offer and concentrates on what individuals achieved in the past.[4] If the future appears to hold fewer opportunities, attention focusses on exploiting what already exists—on protecting jobs, on closing markets, on shunning ideas, on re-distributing income and property. Such a static philosophy of society tends to be self-fulfilling. Disputes over the distribution of present incomes increase rigidities in the economic process and reduce future incomes all round.[5] If, for example, more of the time and energy of employers and employees in Britain could be devoted to increasing productivity and efficiency and less to arguing over the division of a shrinking cake, there could soon be bigger slices for all.[6]

IMPORTANCE OF CULTURE AND ATTITUDES

Considerable research and analysis has been devoted to

15

trying to isolate and assess the important sources of economic growth. The significance of contributions made by natural resources, investment and education have been analysed in some detail. All this, however, has only served to underline that the process is complex and that no single explanation will prove adequate. In fact, the process of economic growth is almost as varied as the cultural, political and economic history of the widely different peoples of the world. Some have found it relatively easy to achieve the accumulation of human and physical resources needed for development. For others that point is still some time away. In general, too much emphasis has been placed on the quantifiable and too little on the intangible (especially culture and attitudes),[7] while the preoccupation with the transfer of resources as a necessary condition promotes the false belief that improvement can be simply a duty of others and not a task for oneself.

Tolstoy pointed out in *War and Peace* that it is possible to assemble statistics about opposing armies, on their numerical strength and material equipment *et cetera*, but the main factors which will decide the outcome of the conflict, namely generalship and the motivation, skill and courage of the soldiers on each side, elude quantification. The same holds in economics. A large part of the variations in rates of growth among countries, whether developed or developing, is accounted for by history, religion, social customs, institutions, modes of thought, motivations and public policies, none of which can be captured by statisticians.

For instance, the motivations of Japanese workers, their distress at criticism, their deference to authority and their close identity with their employer, contrast sharply with some of their Western counterparts. These and other important but intangible factors contribute in large measure to Japanese progress. If they had been absent, external aid and open markets in the world economy

16

could not have created them; and there is no reason to believe the same progress could have been achieved.

The case of Hong Kong, although special, is also instructive. Less than 400 square miles in extent and supporting a population of around 5 million, she is one of the few colonies still in existence. Her only natural resource is a harbour. The government restricts itself to the more traditional functions and, within a legal framework, the hard working, thrifty and entrepreneurial characteristics of the people are given a free rein in a market economy. From an entrepot port, Hong Kong has become in the last two decades the base of some of the largest merchant shipping fleets in the world and a substantial exporting centre, producing a wide range of goods, from cotton yarn to television sets, becoming progressively more sophisticated with the passage of time.

Similar advances have been made by Singapore and they have been made with only token financial aid from abroad. South Korea and Taiwan received substantial foreign aid in the early stages of their development, chiefly for politico-strategic reasons. But as with Singapore, Hong Kong and Japan (and, among others, Malaysia, Thailand and Brazil) much of the explanation for their advancement is to be found in the character, skills and attitudes of their peoples.

ROLE OF PRIVATE ENTERPRISE

Since the international debate on how to promote economic development in the Third World has been conducted almost entirely by representatives of governments and international bureaucrats, this has inevitably meant that the major topics on which discussion has concentrated have been those which are supposedly susceptible to government action.

It is thus not surprising, but certainly regrettable, that the role of private enterprise in economic development has been neglected in inter-governmental deliberations.

Little objective consideration has been given to the real importance of private enterprise—whether as individuals or firms, cooperatives or companies, be they domestic or foreign—in the task of efficiently utilising scarce capital and skills and creating new jobs as part of the development process.

Throughout the non-Communist world, industry and trade is carried on, to an overwhelming extent, by private enterprises; they, not governments or inter-governmental organisations, are the principal engines of wealth creation. The prosperity of Japan and the countries of Western Europe, North America and Australasia is essentially the creation of private initiative. The evidence is there that it is those countries in the Third World that have facilitated and encouraged entrepreneurial endeavours, although exceptions can be cited, which have made the most progress towards industrialisation as the basis for a prosperous economy.

In reviewing the economic performance of developing countries over the last two decades, the World Bank's *World Development Report* for 1981 concludes that 'policies in the successful countries have been generally supportive of industrialisation and commerce, but have avoided directing that support at any particular sector or method. Decisions about what activities and what processes could be efficiently built up are left to individual firms which succeed or fail as their decisions prove to be correct or incorrect.'[8]

Successful development of an economy depends on the success of many different activities—investment, employment creation, the introduction and adaptation of technology, the management of enterprises (which includes both the conduct of human relations and the skills required in the direction of manufacturing operations including the control of materials and quality supervision), the conduct of trade (marketing, distribution, after-sales service) and above all the ability to innovate. In every phase of this process it seems clear that the advantage lies with the decisions of de-centralised private enterprise over any system of centralised bureaucratic control. In a world where a myriad of commercial decisions have to be made every day, in a multitude of circumstances which differ from occasion to occasion, central decisions or directives are most unlikely to be 'better' than those made by individuals or companies whose fortunes depend on whether they are right or wrong. Moreover, the subjection of commercial decisions to bureaucratic control opens the door to excessive political interference and, too, to corruption.

Economic growth involves a continuous adjustment to opportunities which are created by ideas, fresh insights, innovation. Both innovation and individual plans for adjusting to it are ventures entailing risk. Thus the 'policy' for growth consists of allowing people to do what they think will improve their welfare. Their willingness to take the risk need not be doubted as long as the environment is favourable to them—as long as it provides scope for entrepreneurship. The economic growth that 'free' markets have produced in modern times resulted from innovation, adjustment and risk taking. Many of those who lost out one day had the confidence that the next could bring new opportunities; and their willingness to search for them, the market being a search process, in fact produced new opportunities for themselves and for others. In the last analysis, as the young Keynes wrote in *The Economic Consequences of the Peace*, wealth is not so much gold or even strategic raw materials. It is hard work, brains, imagination, initiative . . .[9]

ROLE OF GOVERNMENT

Private enterprise cannot discharge its role successfully, it cannot contribute to the development of an economy, in the face of government wrong-headedness or opposition. This will be especially so in countries with a strong tradition of powerful governmental objectives in social policy or in those newly independent countries which are still feeling their way towards establishing new patterns of social and institutional organisation. This historical distrust of some developing-country governments towards private enterprises, more so in the case of those that are foreign owned, has to be recognised. It must also be recognised, however, that persistence in such distrust and hostility is not the way to learn the skills which private enterprise can provide or to encourage the innovatory function which is the most potent source of progress. For private enterprise to participate fruitfully in the development process requires, at a minimum, a lack of hostility on the part of the government. And an openness and receptiveness to its potentialities is likely to achieve even better results.

Government's impact on the economic environment, whether direct or indirect, is pervasive. In many developing countries can be witnessed an imbalance between resources devoted to planning and those available for productive use. High proportions of educated people, a scarce resource in developing countries, are in government occupations. This disproportion weighs too heavily on young economies. Governments are geared to extracting, not creating, wealth. However able the governors, they cannot extract wealth from those who do not have it.

The task of government is to provide internal conditions of order and stability within which individuals and firms can go about their business in confidence. These 'rules of the road', as Friederick von Hayek has put it, are not to tell people where to go, but to prevent them from getting in one another's way.[10]

A government by its actions can help or retard the process of economic development in a great many ways. There are, first, the steps that it can take to try to ensure a stable social and institutional environment, conducive to development. Is there a high standard of public law and order? Is there a reasonable standard of integrity in government and business? What are the general health conditions? Are population policies conducive to the general increase of welfare among the people? Is the system of land tenure such, or is it being reformed in such a way, as to promote a sound agriculture? Is there an adequate educational system and any system of technical training? What sort of communications infrastructure exists? What are the general attitudes towards commercial activity—such as enforcement of contracts and trademark and patent protection?

Most important, however, will be the considerations arising directly from government economic policy. Is it inclined towards intervention, regulation and control, or towards encouraging competition and facilitating independent enterprise and innovation? What attitudes does the government have towards indigenous industry? Are local industries heavily protected against imports or supported by government subsidy? Is there a high degree of control or direction of investment? What is the record on nationalisation and on compensation in the event of nationalisation? How does the taxation system bear on individuals and on business? Are there controls on prices, wages, profits and dividends? As far as foreign investors are concerned, are there discriminations against them? Are there difficult establishment requirements? Are there restrictions on the sectors open to foreign firms? Are the local subsidiaries of foreign firms treated differently in regard to internal legislation from domestically-owned firms? Are there equitable and reasonable conditions in relation to profit repatriation and local equity participation? Are there adequate and easily accessible channels of communication to ensure the best possible mutual understanding between government and business about their respective roles?

Two aspects of government policy are of such special importance for growth as to merit more detailed consideration: whether development strategies are inward or outward looking; and what is the attitude to foreign direct investment.

Inward- and Outward-looking Strategies

A shift from inward-looking strategies for development, based on import-substitution policies, to outward-looking strategies, based on export-oriented policies, had much to do with the transformation of Brazil, Singapore, South Korea, Taiwan, Hong Kong and others into 'newly industrialising countries'.[11]

Import-substitution policies, differing in detail between countries, are usually based on the premise that industrial growth can occur at a rapid rate only if a country 'de-links' itself from world production and new industries are encouraged to start production everywhere there is a domestic need to be met. Encouragements have included tight protection against imports, either by prohibitively high tariffs or by severe quantitative restrictions; and domestic interventions and controls have also been employed, discriminating between industries. Import-substitution policies have been an important factor in explaining the relatively poor growth performance of the countries which continue to adhere to them. Whatever else might have been intended, they have not been conducive either to high levels of employment and capacity utilisation or to reduced 'dependence' on foreign supplies (including official development assistance). Indeed, these policies led the developing countries to experience declining shares in world trade, which critics of the international system of trade and payments deem to be proof that the system is biased against Third World interests.

The difficulties with such policies can be explained as resulting from rational responses by profit-maximising entrepreneurs to bureaucratic controls rather than to market signals. The difficulties inherent in their adminis-

22

tration indicate something of the problems of moving towards export-oriented policies. First, as domestic industries grow used to protected domestic markets, the entrepreneurs engaged in them are inclined to lobby, individually and collectively, for the maintenance of protection. Secondly, 'rents' accrue to the beneficiaries of import licences, monopoly rights, public subsidies and so on, providing another incentive for business efforts to be diverted into lobbying. Thirdly, even if bureaucratic decisions are formally guided by a plan, they are hardly ever informed by published—and therefore predictable— economic criteria and consequently entrepreneurs face considerable uncertainties in planning new developments. And fourthly, the whole system of controls, administered in a discretionary—and therefore indiscriminate—fashion, creates a bureaucratic vested interest in its continuance.

The *World Development Report* for 1981 observes that 'the successful countries [of the Third World] have been those which have resisted or overcome the temptation to adopt inward-looking trade strategies'; they have not delayed transition to greater export orientation. 'Although some of the successful countries have exploited import substitution at earlier stages of industrialisation (particularly the larger ones such as Brazil),' the report continues, 'they avoid the burdens to exports that extending import substitution to intermediate goods would have entailed and began at an early stage to move away from this orientation.'[12]

A recent authoritative survey of the available evidence on trade and development, covering several major studies, concludes that 'there seems to be a general case . . . for arguing that it is really a shift to successful liberalisation and therefore continuing liberalisation that is critical to improved export performance on a sustained basis'. Later it says 'there is little doubt that . . . the countries that have managed to shift to improved export performance, by reducing export bias, have also managed to register acceleration in their growth rates, whereas countries that have not done so have had poorer growth rates'.[13]

The success of outward-looking strategies, especially in the now middle-income developing countries, has been such that the Secretary-General of the Organisation for Economic Cooperation and Development (OECD) remarked in his report on *The Impact of the Newly Industrialising Countries* that they are likely to be continued or adopted by a growing number of countries in the Third World, provided a reasonably expansionary and open world economy is maintained.[14]

Earlier in the OECD report it was pointed out that what the newly industrialising countries have in common, if to varying degrees, is the emphasis they place on export-oriented policies as a means of promoting rapid industrialisation and on the market mechanism as a means of allocating scarce resources. The success of these policies, the report adds, is largely conditioned by the existence of (i) a disciplined, educated and skilled labour force, (ii) the emergence of an active and efficient entrepreneurial class and (iii) an adequate degree of political stability. And most of them welcome foreign investment.[15]

Foreign Direct Investment

Governments can greatly influence growth by the attitude they adopt to foreign direct investment and to the operations of multi national enterprises. Nearly all the nations now in existence were substantially assisted in their development by foreign investment; and in the developing countries today, at their varying levels of development, different types of foreign investment continue to play a vital role in transferring entrepreneurship, managerial expertise, capital and technology. The annual net flow of private investment to developing countries from the OECD countries showed a continual increase during the 1970s from an average of $2,600 million in 1967-69 to $13,490 million in 1979.[16] Table 2.1 sets out the net external financial receipts of developing countries from all sources from 1970 to 1979 and illustrates the significant flow of direct investment. Much of this investment has been through the agency of the multinational enterprise, the emergence of which has played a critical role in the growth of international trade and capital flows, endowing investment with a high degree of flexibility and adaptability.

The controversies which have surrounded multinational enterprises ought not to obscure the very real benefit which their activities can have for the developing countries. Their entrepreneurial activities have brought to developing countries part of the dynamic entrepreneurial spirit of the developed world. They have found opportunities for creating new and better products from the natural, human and capital resources of the country. They have assembled capital, particularly for the development of natural resources, on a scale beyond the capacity of the local governments and domestic entrepreneurs. Where labour used to the disciplines of a modern industry has been scarce, labour training at all levels has been one of their most important contributions to development. They have also brought management training and demonstrated techniques for combining capital and skills. They have enabled developing countries to market manufactured goods abroad by producing goods up to international quality standards and in adequate supply and, also, in providing distribution outlets in foreign markets.

Most significant recently has been the role of foreign direct investment in the transfer of technology. As a recent study puts it: 'The multinational is the only organisation that will in the near future be capable of generating massive flows of embodied and disembodied "hardware" and "software" technology to the developing countries. In a world where aid and technical assistance programmes are shrinking daily, the multinational will in

TABLE 2.1

Net External Financial Receipts of Developing Countries by Type of Flow, 1970-79

	billion dollars				Share of total in %			
	1970	1974	1978	1979	1970	1974	1978	1979
ODA	8.13	14.94	23.44	27.97	42.6	44.1	29.5	34.6
DAC bilateral	5.67	8.24	13.12	15.91	29.7	24.3	16.5	19.7
OPEC bilateral	0.35	3.02	2.97	4.02	1.8	8.9	3.8	5.0
Multilateral	1.07	2.85	5.99	6.10	5.6	8.4	7.5	7.5
of which: OPEC	—	0.12	0.96	0.25	—	0.4	1.2	0.3
Other	1.04	0.83	1.36	1.94	5.5	2.5	1.7	2.4
of which: CMEA	1.04	0.83	1.26	1.84	5.5	2.5	1.5	2.3
Non-concessional	10.95	18.98	56.16	53.01	57.4	55.9	70.5	65.4
Bank lending	3.00	10.00	22.51	16.67	15.7	29.5	28.3	20.6
Bonds	0.30	0.28	3.03	(3.00)	1.6	0.8	3.8	3.7
Export credits	2.71	3.25	12.93	10.76	14.2	9.4	16.3	13.3
of which: Private	2.16	2.49	9.97	9.42	11.3	7.3	12.6	11.5
Official	0.55	0.70	2.96	1.50	2.9	2.1	3.7	1.8
Direct investment	3.69	1.10[a]	11.15	13.49	19.3	3.3[a]	13.9	16
OPEC bilateral	0.20	0.92	1.02	0.80	1.0	2.7	1.3	1.0

Multilateral	0.69	1.81	3.41	4.20	3.6	5.3	4.3	5.2
of which: OPEC	—	0.02	0.49	(0.30)	—	0.1	0.6	0.4
Other	0.36	1.42	2.11	3.93	{ 1.9	4.8	2.7	4.9
of which: CMEA	0.11	0.09	0.10	0.10	0.6	0.3	0.1	0.1
Total receipts	19.08	33.92	79.60	80.98	100.0	100.0	100.0	100.0
Per cent of GNP	4.0	3.5	5.1	4.6				

SOURCE: *Development Cooperation, 1980 Review* (Paris: OECD Secretariat, 1980) Table IV-8.

[a]Figure significantly below trend because of nationalisation (disinvestment) of major companies' assets by certain oil-exporting countries.

all likelihood increase as the agent of technology transfer to the developing countries.'[17] With their size and command over resources in different parts of the world, multinational enterprises can reap economies of scale in the production and distribution of knowledge. Their geographical dispersion and ability to follow a common strategy allow them to share the costs and benefits of their activities between the countries in which they operate.

Developing countries should utilise fully the proven abilities of multinational enterprises as conduits for the transfer of technology. The relative costs involved in foreign direct investment are likely to be less than those of the alternatives. If the objective is to use labour efficiently there are good grounds for believing that, if the incentives and opportunities are provided, multinational enterprises are likely to adopt cost-minimising labour-intensive technologies. As long as governments are well-informed and resolute as well as fair-minded in their dealings, they should be able to ensure that their economy and their people gain from the activities of multinational enterprises.[18]

Many of the criticisms of the operations of multinational enterprises have less substance than might have been imagined from the sound and fury they generate.[19] The basic point is that these concentrations of managerial and technical expertise are profit oriented, which means it is not appropriate to criticise them as if they were aid agencies; but because they are profit oriented they will make their abilities available in response to intelligent policy making. Thus much of the criticism of multinational enterprises is better directed at the interventions of host governments to secure their entry into high-technology sectors and often to keep them out of other sectors.

Multinational enterprises must be seen in the context of developments that have been taking place outside the inter-governmental organisations in the field of foreign investment. Ideological prejudice and nationalism still persist, but there has been much change in attitudes on the part of both governments and private industry over the last decade. Among the manifestations of these changes are the rapidly increasing use of bilateral treaties for the promotion and protection of investments (there are now almost 200 such treaties including a substantial number negotiated during the last two years) and increasing recognition of the value of, and the need for, international arbitration through established organisations and under agreed international rules. In fact, some of these treaties are between two developing countries, which shows that the governments concerned are interested in the protection of their own companies operating in other developing countries.

Going far beyond this is the increased flexibility and adaptability which is being shown both by many governments and by business. In particular, many new forms of investment have become common in addition to the classic form in which the foreign investor controlled his investment through a wholly-owned subsidiary. There are certainly still many cases where the interests both of the investor and of the development prospects of the developing country will be best served in this way—and this is often so recognised. But the range of alternative possibilities is now very large, including joint ventures, production-sharing contracts (particularly in extractive industries), franchise agreements and service contracts (including management agreements) in which the foreign partner may or may not hold some equity participation. Both sides must make their own calculation of the costs involved in pursuing the courses available; and in many cases, the balance of the calculation will depend on a trade-off between efficiency and political considerations. In some cases it also turns out that governments of developing countries compete with each other in providing excessively generous incentives to foreign investors and thus forgoing potential benefits. A reversal of such 'generosity' seems feasible, however, since all available evidence indicates that the decision to invest in a particular country does not critically depend on the financial incentives given by the host government.

Once this calculation about forms of investment has been made, it remains true that private enterprise will operate most efficiently, and will make its maximum contribution to the country's development, in a competitive and open market and in an environment which welcomes its activity and recognises its value. This applies also to domestic investors.

CHOICE FOR PUBLIC POLICY

To sum up, a review of the sources of growth indicates the possible diversity and divergence of conditions which exist from one country to another. Apart from the cultural conditions and resources of a country, many of the conditions that shape development, and especially the contribution of private enterprise, depend on and are within the will of the government of the country concerned. In most of these matters, the internal policies of governments are decisive; and the external influence of 'transfers of resources', either through official aid or through distortions of the market process, play a relatively minor role.

The corollary of this proposition is that the government of a developing country has a choice in its own hands. It is certainly within the sovereign power of any government to choose not to use private enterprise to mobilise its national skills and resources. Similarly it has every right to refuse foreign firms or individuals little or any part in its country's development. But the exercise of these rights entails costs. It is of primary importance that the price paid by the country, in terms of rejected experience, skills and ability, and hence in terms of higher income for its inhabitants, should be appreciated. And it should not be taken for granted that such costs can be 'externalised' in the sense that other countries have to bear them. To put it in another way, every country has the right to social experiment, but at its own expense.

NOTES AND REFERENCES

1.A popular exposition of this view can be found in Lester C. Thurow, *The Zero-sum Society: Distribution and the Possibilities for Economic Change* (New York: Basic Books, 1980; and Harmondsworth: Penguin Books, 1981).

2.This approach is disposed of in Harry G. Johnson, *Technology and Economic Interdependence* (London: Macmillan, for the Trade Policy Research Centre, 1975).

3.Richard Blackhurst, Nicolas Marian and Jan Tumlir, *Adjustment, Trade and Growth in Developed and Developing Countries*, GATT Studies in International Trade No. 6 (Geneva: GATT Secretariat, 1978), p. 67.

4.Giersch, 'On the Future of the World Economy: an Optimist's View', *The World Economy*, London, September 1979.

5.In concentrating on job retention instead of job creation, no society could ever maintain the previous levels achieved.

6.Scott, Corden and Little, *The Case against General Import Restrictions*, Thames Essay No. 24 (London: Trade Policy Research Centre, 1980), p. 78.

7.The point is developed in Lord McFadzean of Kelvinside, 'Market Forces and "Those Who Foretell the Future ... " ', *The World Economy*, March 1981.

8.*World Development Report 1981* (Washington: World Bank, 1981), p. 26.

9.John Maynard Keynes, *The Economic Consequences of the Peace* (London: Macmillan, 1920).

10.'The distinction ... between formal law or justice and substantive rules is very important and at the same time most difficult to draw in practice. Yet the general principle involved is simple enough. The difference between the two kinds of rules is the same as that between laying down a Rule of the Road, as in the Highway Code, and ordering people where to go; or, better still, between providing signposts and commanding people which road to take.' See F. A. Hayek, *Road to Serfdom*, revised edition (London: Routledge & Kegan Paul, 1976), pp. 55-56.

11.The principal studies have been reported in the following publications: Little, Scitovsky and Scott, *Industry and Trade in Some Developing Countries: a Comparative Study, op. cit.*; Bela Balassa, *et al.*, *The Structure of Protection in Developing Countries* (Baltimore: Johns Hopkins Press, for the World Bank, 1971); Balassa, 'Export Incentives and Export Performance in Developing Countries: a Comparative Study', *Weltwirtschaftliches Archiv*, Kiel, Vol. 114, No. 3, 1978; Anne O. Krueger, *Foreign Trade Regimes and Economic Development: Liberalization Attempts and Consequences* (Cambridge, Mass.: Ballinger, for the National Bureau of Economic Research, 1978); Krueger, 'Alternative Trade Strategies and Employment in LDCs', *American Economic Review*

(Papers and Proceedings), Menasha, May 1978; and Jagdish Bhagwati, *Foreign Trade Regimes and Economic Development: Anatomy and Consequences of Exchange Control Regimes* (Cambridge, Mass.: Ballinger, for the National Bureau of Economic Research, 1979).

The results of a project carried out at the Institut für Weltwirtschaft, in the Federal Republic of Germany, are summarised in the following: Donges, 'A Comparative Survey of Industrialisation Policies in Fifteen Semi-industrial Countries', *Weltwirtschaftliches Archiv*, Vol. 112, No. 4, 1976; Donges and James Riedel, 'The Expansion of Manufactured Exports in Developing Countries: an Empirical Assessment of Supply and Demand Issues', *Weltwirtschaftliches Archiv*, Vol. 113, No. 1, 1977; and Donges and Lotte Muller-Ohlsen, *Aussenwirtschaftsstrategien und Industrialisierung in Entwicklungslandern* (Tübingen: J. C. B. Mohr, for the Institut für Weltwirtschaft an der Universität Kiel, 1978).

Also see, Donges, 'Trade for Development', a paper prepared for the Study Group.

12.*World Development Report 1981, op. cit.*, p. 25.

13.Bhagwati and T. N. Srinivasan, *International Economic Policy: Theory and Evidence* (Baltimore: Johns Hopkins Press, 1979), pp. 16 and 17.

14.Secretary General of the OECD, *The Impact of the Newly Industrialising Countries* (Paris: OECD Secretariat, 1979), p. 14.

15.*Ibid.*, p. 11.

16.*Development Cooperation* (Paris: OECD Secretariat, 1980), Table IV-8.

17.Hans Singer and Javed Ansari, *Rich and Poor Countries* (London: Allen & Unwin, 1977), p. 209.

18.V. N. Balasubramanyam, 'Technology for Development', a paper for the Study Group.

19.For a succinct review of the criticism of the operations of multinational enterprises, see Balasubramanyam, *Multinational Enterprises and the Third World*, Thames Essay No. 26 (London: Trade Policy Research Centre, 1980).

CHAPTER THREE

Essentials of the International Economic Order

JUST as a stable institutional environment is required for private enterprise to flourish at national level, so such an environment is necessary at international level, entailing the achievement and maintenance of open markets and well-defined rules for regulating the behaviour of governments. Such an international order was established in the aftermath of World War II. As a consequence, and although poverty persists in many parts of the world, the growth of world trade and prosperity since the 1940s has been, by all historical standards, quite exceptional. It would therefore be prudent, before accepting that there is a need for a 'new international economic order', to examine why the present order took the form it did and on what rules it was expected to rest.

In the middle of World War II, the United States and the United Kingdom were already discussing the institutional arrangements through which, on the return to peace, orderly conditions in international trade and payments might be restored and checks established against the manifestations of economic nationalism which had contributed to the outbreak of hostilities.[1] As the war was drawing to an end representatives of the allied governments, meeting in Bretton Woods in the United States, sought agreement on a durable framework of principles and rules for maintaining monetary stability and reforming the autarkic and discriminatory policies which, with governments heavily involved in national economies, were the result of the protectionist excesses of the 1930s. In looking ahead, they had to look back, right back to what happened after World War I.

Today it is hard to imagine the weight of uncertainty that pressed on anyone who had to exercise responsibility in business or government in the inter-war period. It was a world in which economic crises and recessions appeared periodically, as unavoidable as natural disasters, going from bad to worse. Firms which survived the last crisis could well perish in the next.[2]

The 1930s are remembered for the Great Depression and the attendant misery of high unemployment. How a normal and expectable recession turned into a financial crisis in 1929 and eventually into a monetary crisis is too complicated a story to relate here.[3] But governmental failures, including the policies of the Federal Reserve System of the United States, played a decisive role.

Besides a wholesale resort to protectionist measures, instability in foreign-exchange markets had also obstructed trade, with competitive devaluations, discriminatory exchange controls and the blocking of currencies. As the world emerged from the Great Depression in 1933 the value of world trade had fallen to a quarter of its 1929 level. By then international trade had been confronted with high tariffs, a myriad of non-tariff restrictions, bilateral pacts, wider preferential agreements and innumerable cartels.

Whatever short-term gains they yielded, the beggar-my-neighbour measures of the 1930s served only to deprive international trade of a stable basis and, by diminishing its volume, to impoverish people everywhere, especially in countries highly dependent on exports.

INSTITUTIONS OF THE ORDER

What was envisaged was an international economic order with two sets of rules, one for trade and one for payments (or international monetary arrangements). It was visualised

(a) that the trade rules, in facilitating trade liberalisation, would ensure non-discrimination in trade relations between countries and would limit the instruments of protection to tariffs, which would be bound against unilateral increases, and

(b) that the monetary rules would introduce and then maintain the convertibility of currencies as an indispensable prerequisite not only for trade but also for capital movements.

It was appreciated that the two sets of rules would have to be closely interrelated because the techniques of trade restrictions and payments restrictions are to a large extent interchangeable.

Once the two sets of rules were in force, with currency convertibility and price stability achieved in the major trading nations and with all participating countries having equal access to the markets of the major trading nations, there could be said to exist an integrated world market. World-market prices could convey to all participants accurate information about investment opportunities and supplies in relation to demand for particular products, enabling the possibility of scarcities or surpluses in the world economy to be anticipated, enabling adjustments to be made in national economies in a timely and orderly way, thereby achieving a degree of stability that could make progress in economic development possible.

IMF to Stabilise Payments

It was in this frame of thought that the Bretton Woods conference established the International Monetary Fund to ensure a stable system of international payments. It provided a pool of gold and currency reserves to meet emergencies, such as payments difficulties occasioned by a fall in export earnings or problems over the servicing of loans, each member country being assigned a quota determining (i) its obligation to contribute to the pool and (ii) its right to draw on the pool.[4] It included rules on the obligations of countries to permit transfers. While it was based on fixed rates of exchange, related to the American dollar, the IMF provided for exchange-rate changes when an economy's balance of payments was in fundamental disequilibrium.

World Bank for Development

The conference at Bretton Woods also established the World Bank in part to assist the reconstruction of war-torn Europe. In the event, the Marshall Plan, with the United States and Canada as donors, was the vehicle for that purpose among the countries belonging to the Organisation for European Economic Cooperation (OEEC). The role of the World Bank was to provide long-term credit on somewhat better than commercial terms, providing a stabilising influence in the revival of private capital markets. In due course its exclusive function came to be the provision of development assistance to less advanced economies.[5]

GATT Rules of Trade

The discussions on the set of rules covering trade, the other side of the international economic order, were much more prolonged. In place of the originally-intended International Trade Organisation (ITO), the General Agreement on Tariffs and Trade, incorporating the proposed ITO's trade policy provisions, came into force in 1948.[6] Thus the GATT became the instrument for regulating the institutional environment of international trade. Its aims were 'the substantial reduction of tariffs and other barriers to trade' and 'the elimination of discriminatory treatment in international commerce'.

The GATT is squarely based on market principles. Only competition can establish a price mechanism through which economically relevant information is promptly communicated. That was partly why the tariff, a device compatible with the price mechanism, was prescribed as the sole instrument for protecting an industry (if necessary). It would protect the industry without isolating it completely from international competition. Another part of the purpose was to make the extent and cost of the protection clearly expressed in the level of the tariff—to make the system of protection 'transparent'.

Because of the disastrous experience with the discriminatory policies and practices of the 1930s, the principle of non-discrimination, set out in Article I, was made the cornerstone of the GATT. It requires all signatory countries to extend most-favoured-nation treatment—in plain language 'equal' treatment—*unconditionally* to all other signatory countries except where, under conditions laid down in Article XXIV, a customs union or free trade area is being formed.[7]

ACHIEVEMENTS OF THE ORDER

Under the institutions established after World War II, the liberalisation of trade and capital movements was a principal contributor to an eight-fold increase in the volume of world trade (1946-80), expanding more rapidly than the growth of world output and income, especially in the 1950s and 1960s.[8] Under them the market-oriented economies were able to recover from the disintegration of the 1930s and 1940s because, *inter alia*, they provided scope for private enterprise to flourish. Table 3.1 sets out figures illustrating the growth of world trade by value and Table 3.2 the growth of trade between the developed and developing countries.

The rapid integration of the world economy has resulted in a high level of interdependence between national economies—especially between the more industrialised ones. Intense competition, large-scale capital flows, technological advances in industry and agriculture,

TABLE 3.1

Growth of World Trade, 1948-80

(billion dollars f.o.b.)

	1948	1960	1970	1980
World exports	55	128	312	1,985
Index 1948 = 100	100	232	567	3,609

SOURCE: *International Trade* (Geneva: GATT Secretariat, various issues.)

TABLE 3.2

Trade between the Developed and Developing Countries 1963-80

(billion dollars f.o.b.)

	1963	1968	1973	1978	1980
Exports from developed[a] to developing countries	23	32	72	206	292
Exports from developing to developed countries	23	32	81	218	378

SOURCE: *International Trade 1980/81* (Geneva: GATT Secretariat, 1981).

[a]North America, Japan, Western Europe, Australia, New Zealand and South Africa.

as well as in transport and communications, international migration of labour, still greater economies of scale and the development of new and expanding markets and of new and cheaper sources of supply of both raw materials and finished goods are all factors that have had, and are having, profound and continuing effects on international trade and production patterns. And the effects are not any more confined to the developed countries. They can be seen spreading to the developing ones and will continue to do so provided the integration of the world economy progresses.

In view of these developments, it was only to be expected that, with the international division of labour becoming a strong feature of the world economy, private enterprise would organise production on an increasingly international basis. The fears which this trend caused at first are, as remarked earlier, giving way to a more balanced evaluation. Indeed, as developing countries become more export oriented, they are themselves beginning to build multinational enterprises.

ESSENCE OF THE ORDER

In essence, then, the international economic order has been based on a dynamic concept of economic activity. The pre-condition of such dynamism was seen as a stable multilateral system of exchange to promote specialisation. Total income is then continually raised by the rising productivity of individuals and groups able to take advantage of the ever growing opportunities for efficient investment and the generation, diffusion and assimilation of knowledge.

The order has provided a stable institutional environment in which economic development can proceed as smoothly as possible. In the long period of prosperity which followed World War II, international trade and investment, it has been noted, were growing much faster than world output and income. The pattern has been so consistent that it is possible to argue that, even for economies with relatively small export sectors, progress in international specialisation is a causative condition of domestic economic growth.

International transactions, being affected by the policies of numerous governments, are exposed to a higher degree of uncertainty than strictly domestic business. For most of the period since World War II, the uncertainty associated with international transactions was effectively constrained, as far as the developed countries were concerned at any rate, by the principles and rules of the international economic order, perhaps by those of the GATT most of all. Their observance by governments helped private enterprise by making predictable those conditions relevant to business decisions which are determined or influenced by government policies. Three points should be noted.

First, international trade rules constrain government intervention in the market so that firms, knowing where they stand *vis-à-vis* their government and the governments of other countries, can conduct their business in a reasonably stable institutional environment. Their planning for expansion or, if need be, for adjustment is therefore greatly facilitated.

Secondly, the same rules enable governments to resist the pressures of sectional interests seeking special treatment—through protective tariffs or non-tariff forms of public assistance[9]—by referring to international obligations that have been accepted to promote wider interests.

Thirdly, the observance of GATT principles and rules restricted the objectives that could be pursued by governments, as well as the instruments for achieving them. The observance of these limitations by all gave each government secure knowledge of what could be expected in the way of policy conduct in other countries. Paradoxically, therefore, the acceptance by governments of constraints on their actions was the pre-condition for them knowing that permitted objectives could be pursued without nullifying, or conflicting with, activity elsewhere.

In brief, international trade rules proscribing certain types of policy, on the one hand, and prescribing certain policy actions in specified circumstances, on the other, are a condition for the effective conduct of policy by each government in exactly the same way that municipal law, constraining the conduct of citizens within its jurisdiction, makes foresight and planning possible for each individual.[10]

Interests of Small Countries

What is important to understand about the international economic order established after World War II is that, for the first time, relations between countries were organised on a rule-oriented basis. It represented a deliberate and conscious effort to make multilateral consultation and negotiation the method, and multilateral institutions the fora, for advancing the economic interest of individual countries in ways promoting the growth of the world economy as a whole.[11]

This applied not only to international economic relations but also, to a much greater degree than ever before, to domestic policies which affected other countries. It is not suggested that countries were willing to subject their domestic decisions, even on matters of vital concern to others, to international jurisdiction and control beyond what was actually covered in the GATT and IMF articles. Among the major trading nations, however, even if with varying degrees of conviction, it was accepted that a framework of principles and rules was in both the general and the particular interest; and that the framework should be reinforced by a formal system—and, better, a general habit—of multilateral discussion and cooperation. In the 1950s and 1960s, virtually any trade matter of interest to two countries was generally regarded as being, directly or indirectly, of interest to all. Two points need to be stressed.

First and foremost, multilateral institutions, like the GATT and the IMF, are nothing if they cannot safeguard the legitimate interests, and enjoy the confidence, of small countries—and by 'small' is meant small in political terms, developed and developing.

The second point is that stable, orderly and predictable economic relations between the major trading powers—and today that means, mainly, the United States, Japan and the European Community —are another necessary condition for international economic order. Indeed, the maintenance of stable, orderly and predictable economic relations between the major trading powers is the most valuable contribution they could make to the development of small countries. But the maintenance of stable, orderly and predictable economic relations between the major trading powers will be impossible if current conceptions of economic policy continue to hold sway in the major capitals of the world.

GRIEVANCES WITH THE OPERATION OF THE SYSTEM OF RULES

At the outset of this report, it was acknowledged that there are legitimate grievances with the operation of the international economic order, although they are not confined to developing countries. The most substantial grievances are with the way in which the GATT system has worked in practice.

First, the principle of non-discrimination, the cornerstone of the GATT system, has been seriously eroded in a number of ways. Preferential trade arrangements, falling far short of satisfying the conditions set out in Article XXIV for departures from the principle to form customs unions and free trade areas, have been proliferating.[12] In addition, there has been a renewed trend towards bilateralism with the proliferation of 'voluntary' export-restraint agreements, which have been negotiated mainly with the industries of developing countries, but also with Japan.

Second, since negotiations on the liberalisation of international trade are conducted on a reciprocal basis, negotiating efforts have concentrated on liberalising trade in products of export interest to developed countries. Developing countries have claimed after each 'round' of multilateral trade negotiations that little progress has been made in expanding market access for products of export interest to them, although this has not prevented an extremely rapid growth in their exports to developed countries. All the same, while import quotas have largely been eliminated on non-agricultural products traded among developed countries, many have been retained by developed countries on goods supplied by developing countries, in spite of efforts by the latter to get them removed.

Thirdly, since the early 1950s trade in temperate-zone agricultural products has been effectively removed from the governance of the GATT, which has meant that the process of trade liberalisation has made little impact on the rising trend of protection accorded to the farm communities of the developed countries.[13] While this issue has been a major concern to the traditional agricultural exporting countries, it is increasingly becoming a concern of developing countries, which also have an interest in agricultural trade (with cereals, oilseeds, meats and sugar exports).[14]

Fourthly, the provision in the GATT permitting emergency protection to be imposed against a sudden surge of imports of a particular product, namely Article XIX, has proved to be inoperable.[15] Governments have found it easier to take liberties with the rules and go outside the GATT altogether. Not only have 'voluntary' export-restraint agreements resulted, but also orderly marketing arrangements, the most conspicuous being the arrangements that have covered trade in textiles and clothing since the early 1960s (the Multi-fibre Arrangement being the present one[16]). The bulk of these agreements impinge on developing-country trade, but the developed countries have also gone outside the GATT framework to resolve trade problems among themselves, as with steel and automobiles.

Fifthly, the 'complaints and arbitration' procedures of the GATT have been, at least until recently, fairly ineffective and consequently small countries have had little prospect of securing satisfaction in trade disputes, especially with the major trading powers.[17]

NOTES AND REFERENCES

1.Authoritative analyses of the economic policies of the 1930s can be found in Heinz W. Arndt, *The Economic Lessons of the Nineteen Thirties* (Oxford: Clarendon Press, 1942) and Lionel Robbins, *The Economic Causes of War* (London: Macmillan, 1942).

2.*Commercial Policy in the Interwar Period: International Proposals and National Policies* (Geneva: League of Nations, 1942); and William E. Rappard, *Postwar Efforts for Freer Trade* (Geneva: Geneva Research Centre, 1938).

3.Charles P. Kindleberger, *The World Depression 1929-1939* (Harmondsworth: Penguin Books, 1973).

4.Richard N. Gardner, *Sterling-Dollar Diplomacy*, 2nd edition (New York: McGraw-Hill, 1969). In the opinion of many, the IMF was always too small for its supposed purposes and, in any case, it hardly operated until the late 1950s.

5.Edward H. Mason and R. E. Asher, *The World Bank since Bretton Woods* (Washington: Brookings Institution, 1973).

6.William Adams Brown, *The United States and the Restoration of World Trade: an Analysis and Appraisal of the ITO Charter and the General Agreement on Tariffs and Trade* (Washington: Brookings Institution, 1950); Gerard Curzon, *Multilateral Commercial Diplomacy* (London: Michael Joseph, 1965); Karin Kock, *International Trade Policy and the GATT 1947-1967* (Stockholm: Almqvist & Wiksell, 1969); John H. Jackson, *World Trade and the Law of the GATT* (Indianapolis: Bobbs-Merrill, 1969); and Kenneth W. Dam, *The GATT Law and International Economic Organization* (Chicago and London: University of Chicago Press, 1970).

7.The other main exception to the MFN principle provides for existing preferential trade arrangements (Article I, paragraph 2).

8.Blackhurst, 'The Outlook for World Trade', *Business Economist*, London, Summer 1981.

9.Robert E. Baldwin, *Non-Tariff Distortions of International Trade* (Washington: Brookings Institution 1970); Curzon and Victoria Curzon, *Hidden Barriers to International Trade*, Thames Essay No. 1 (London: Trade Policy Research Centre, 1970); Corden and Gerhard Fels, *Public Assistance to Industry* (London: Macmillan, for the Trade Policy Research Centre and the Institut für Weltwirtschaft an der Universität Kiel, 1976); and Harald B. Malmgren, *International Order for Public Subsidies*, Thames Essay No. 11 (London: Trade Policy Research Centre, 1977).

10. Hugh Corbet, 'What Happens after the Tokyo Round Negotiations', *Asia Pacific Community*, Tokyo, Spring 1979.

11. In this connection, see Albert O. Hirschman, *National Power and the Structure of Foreign Trade* (Berkeley and Los Angeles: University of California Press, 1945).

12. This development is associated with the growth of preferential trading arrangements centred on the European Community. See Sir Alec Cairncross, Giersch, Alexander Lamfalussy, Giuseppe Petrilli and Pierre Uri, *Economic Policy for the European Community: the Way Forward* (London: Macmillan, for the Institut für Weltwirtschaft an der Universität Kiel, 1974).

13. D. Gale Johnson, *World Agriculture in Disarray* (London: Macmillan, for the Trade Policy Research Centre, 1973).

14. This is being demonstrated in disputes being brought to GATT attention by developing countries.

15. David Robertson, *Fail Safe Systems for Trade Liberalisation*, Thames Essay No. 12 (London: Trade Policy Research Centre, 1977).

16. For a comprehensive analysis of the MFA, see Donald B. Keesing and Martin Wolf, *Textile Quotas against Developing Countries*, Thames Essay No. 23 (London: Trade Policy Research Centre, 1980).

17. The issue is analysed in Robert E. Hudec, *Adjudication of International Trade Disputes*, Thames Essay No. 16 (London: Trade Policy Research Centre, 1978).

CHAPTER FOUR

Threats to the International Economic Order

SINCE the early 1960s, the international economic order, as well as the market economy at national level, has come under assault—directly and indirectly. The developed countries have generally claimed to adhere to the liberal principles of the international economic order, but in their actions, often motivated by short-term pragmatism, they have been undermining them. Moreover, some of the objectives of policy that have come to the fore, over the past two decades, strike at the roots of an open world economy. The developing countries, in the meantime, have claimed that the liberal principles of the international economic order are either irrelevant to their interests or actually harmful. Their demands for a 'new international economic order' therefore amount to a powerful direct assault on the present framework of principles and rules. As a result of these developments, the legitimacy of the international economic order is being undermined directly and, in addition, its workings are being impaired, thus undermining its legitimacy indirectly.

ASSAULT OF DEVELOPED COUNTRIES

The assault on the international economic order is dangerous because, above all other considerations, there is no coherent alternative. The principles and rules of the international system of trade and payments, as established after World War II, were based on the experience of centuries of commercial diplomacy and on a body of economic theory, originally and essentially concerned with economic growth, that had been developed over a couple of hundred years. Unfortunately, even where there is acceptance of the principles of the international economic order, as in most of the developed countries, the economic policies of governments hardly ever draw systematically on economic theory, for they are intrinsically responses to particular situations. In the political or decision-making process the tendency is for situations to be settled 'on their merits' or 'by common sense'. But they are often not well settled on that basis. Their merits can really only be discerned by reference to theoretical principles. Dispensing with theoretical principles all too frequently means that economic decision making becomes self-defeating *ad hoc*kery.

Under-estimation of Market Forces

Notwithstanding the market principles of the international economic order, and of the GATT in particular, there has been since the 1960s an increasing degree of government intervention in the market process of the market-oriented economies. The issue of state intervention versus market forces is hardly new. It was, after all, the focus of *The Wealth of Nations*.[1] It exercised Keynes in the 1930s. He argued that since market forces could not be relied on to maintain an economy in equilibrium at full employment there should be government expenditure to expand aggregate demand until full employment was achieved.[2] The compelling Keynesian explanation of the business cycle, and the ensuing sense of mastery over it, induced after World War II a sense of social exuberance which was, perhaps, understandable. As the 1950s gave way to the 1960s, it gradually came to be believed, with stable and growing prosperity (among the developed countries), that anything a society thought desirable could be attained.

Widespread confidence that all the main economic problems could be handled had an impact on social attitudes, making for changes in expectations, which slowly came to influence policy.[3] In response to rising expectations, communicated through electoral pressures, governments began to assume more and more responsibilities towards the social and economic welfare of their peoples. Thus the commitment to full employment came to be interpreted, in some countries, as a commitment not only for every man to be employed, but for him to be employed in the occupation of his choice, in the location of his choice and, it has sometimes seemed, at the income of his choice.[4]

Responsibilities have been assumed by governments not only for full employment but for economic growth, income redistribution and price stability; and, beyond greater equality in general, specific income and price guarantees to particular sections of society—notably the farm community. Still further responsibilities have been assumed through policies for regional balance in economic development, for environmental control and for industrial organisation, involving the promotion of high-technology industries (and the protection of low-technology ones), the 'encouragement' of exports and the regulation of investment flows.

What has happened, in sum, is that the Keynesian insight has been seriously misinterpreted. The idea that a free economy has a permanent tendency towards under-employment of resources has led to a general loss of confidence in the market process or to an inclination, at least, to under-estimate the importance of market forces.[5] What have been the consequences?

Consequences of Government Intervention
When government objectives become so numerous that

48

a policy in pursuit of one objective affects the attainment of several or many others, policy making becomes more complex and the outcome and duration of any particular policy becomes less easy to anticipate, whether for those making policy or for those affected by it. A likely effect is a decrease in the efficiency and speed of both public and private decision making, making for rigidities in the structures of the economies of the developed countries, thus impairing the ability of those countries to maintain growth.

The tendency to under-rate the capabilities of the market, with too much made of market imperfections, has provided the basis for much government intervention. All too often, government measures have been introduced to postpone, to 'correct' or to offset adjustment to changing circumstances. Albeit for social reasons, governments have been acting more and more as receivers in attempts to husband industries no longer able to cope, in both home and third-country markets, with more dynamic competition from elsewhere in the world. So-called industrial policies, effected through non-tariff measures, ranging from subsidies and discriminatory public procurement through to 'voluntary' export-restraint agreements and cartel or cartel-like arrangements,[6] have been multiplying since the late 1960s—a phenomenon which has come to be known as 'neo-protectionism'.[7]

As with neo-protectionist measures, weakening trends in growth of productivity observable in most developed countries[8] are due, if only partly, to resistance to pressure for structural change stemming from technological innovations and shifts in comparative advantage—to a refusal, in the final analysis, to accept cheaper imports and adjust to them. It cannot be disputed that the process of structural adjustment in the developed countries, necessary to accommodate not only continuing demands for economic growth in them but also rising expectations in developing countries, is not proceeding at all well.

Inflation is both a symptom and a cause of these growing structural rigidities.[9]

It is a symptom because inflation emerges when macro-economic policy aims at the achievement of a level of employment and activity that micro-economic rigidities preclude.

It is a cause because inflation, in turn, impairs the efficiency of the market mechanism.

These losses in efficiency result from increased uncertainty about the relative price movements that underlie general price inflation. Increased resources must then be devoted to finding out the relevant information. Costs arise also because of the reduction in, and misallocation of, investments which inevitably follows from price confusion. Furthermore, inflation contributes to international monetary disorder, which makes relative price movements still more uncertain, and distorts international capital flows towards countries and currencies offering greater stability, causing problems in domestic monetary management.

Inflation is a direct threat as well to international stability. Societies attempting to live with inflation soon disintegrate into interest groups organised for self-defence. National governments become preoccupied with maintaining internal cohesion at the expense of international cooperation. Thus monetary order, the maintenance of stable purchasing power, is a crucial prerequisite for sustained growth. This, however, depends on mastering inflation without chronic recession and sluggish demand—something that no developed country has yet been able to do, although some come a great deal closer than others. Yet without such success, recession will be endemic, while political pressures for protection will be almost irresistible.

Turning to another set of consequences, the encroachment of government into the allocation of resources has given rise to the easy politics of 'pluralism', which entails building political majorities by aggregating different and distinct sections of society with promises to 'do something' about each group's special interest. Pluralistic politics, however, do not entail a consistent conception of how those disparate sectional interests might be reconciled, let alone reconciled to the public interest.

By assuming a responsibility, a government virtually creates the pressure group that will expect it to exercise that responsibility. In the process it will excite mutually incompatible expectations. But a government which resolutely took the attitude that it had no power to act effectively would have a consistent answer to the pressures put upon it. Once a government claims powers it will be hard to explain why it does not use them in the service of the sectional interests affected.

It is evident, then, that many of the responsibilities assumed by governments have been far more easily undertaken than discharged. This has become plain at international level where, with the growing inter-dependence of national economies, governments are finding external obligations increasingly in conflict with internal ones. Not only do a given government's inter-ventions conflict with one another within the national economy; the policies of governments also conflict internationally.[10] Economic measures in one country are liable to affect economic conditions in other countries, provoking reactions from the affected interests in those countries, thereby making for international friction.[11]

Thus the exercise of sovereignty over domestic economic affairs can be seen to conflict with the benefits that have resulted from the movement, over the last three decades, towards an open world economy. The governments of the developed countries have each tried to retain a degree of freedom of national action which, in an interdependent world, produces an increasing incompatibility with the maintenance of an international economic order.[12]

The decline in the efficiency of the economies of the developed countries and the impairment of the international economic order have both direct and indirect consequences for the developing countries. The immediate effect is that discriminatory protection, which has been an alternative to adjustment, is itself a prime case of abandonment of GATT principles and has frequently been directed against the more successful of the developing countries. The indirect effect comes *via* the reduction in overall economic growth in developed countries, which exacerbates protectionist pressures and constricts market opportunities for the exports of developing countries.

It is right to focus on the role of developed countries in impairing the international economic order, for it embodies their principles, it is their creation and it ultimately depends on their adherence. Nevertheless, the underlying philosophy of the developing countries, as exemplified in the demands for a 'new international economic order', have made an important negative contribution. The Brandt Report itself is a spokesman of considerable eloquence for these positions.

Market Forces and Inequality

The assault on the liberal principles of the existing international economic order by spokesmen for the developing countries has at its roots a profound suspicion of the efficiency and equity of the market process. This has been accompanied by a preoccupation with relative poverty as between countries and individuals rather than with the central problem of the absolute poverty of far too many people in the developing countries. No better statement of the suspicion of the equity of market forces exists than in the Brandt Report, which states that 'in the world, as in nations, economic forces left entirely to themselves produce growing inequality'.[11] In spite of its far-reaching implications, no attempt is made to prove this startling assertion; it is accepted as a self-evident truth. But it is by no means self-evident, either as between nations or within nations.

As between nations, examples abound of relatively poor countries working themselves up to a status of relative affluence and overtaking, in the process, other countries which have been considered affluent and powerful. In Europe before World War II, Germany was a poor country relative to the United Kingdom, Switzerland, Sweden and France. Southern Europe, in particular, was poor relative to Northern Europe; but Spain, Portugal, Italy and Greece have, over the post-war period, shown higher per capita and aggregate rates of growth than the rest of Western Europe. Western Europe as a whole has virtually evened the income gap between itself and North America where poorer Canada has been growing more rapidly than the richer United States of America. Japan, Hong Kong, Brazil, South Korea and Taiwan are only the vanguard of yet another wave of industrialisation. If the analysis in this report is near the mark, many more developing countries would have been catching up more rapidly, had they better exploited market forces. Indeed, it could be argued that the statement in the Brandt Report quoted above is the reverse of the truth.

Moreover, if market forces left to themselves can be relied on to produce cumulative inequality, what have the developed countries to fear in commercial competition with the developing world? And how is to be explained the resurgence of protectionism in developed countries over the last decade and a half, so much of it directed in an explicitly discriminatory fashion against the developing countries?

Within the developing countries (as within the developed countries) there are of course great inequalities of income. But many of these inequalities spring not from market forces but from the intervention of governments in the economy in the form, for example, of import-substitution policies, concentration on capital-intensive/ high-wage industries and controls leading to corruption.

In any case, either as between societies or within societies, it is absurd to suggest that the rich only become richer at the expense of the poor. A barber in Frankfurt performs broadly the same service for the community as his opposite numbers in London and Djakarta, yet he enjoys a higher standard of living than his British equivalent; and both of them enjoy more of the world's goods than the Indonesian barber. This is the result of the operation of normal market forces. The poor associated with the rich are richer than the poor associated with the poorer. Where there is an expanding economy with growing employment opportunities, there comes a point in economic development when unskilled labour becomes relatively scarce and demand pulls its wages up. In brief, there is a dynamic linking. Migrant labour did not flock to West Germany and other developed countries because the poor in these economies were becoming poorer.

Demands for a New Order

The prevalence of these views about market forces is perhaps more important than their lack of truth. The questioning of market solutions certainly runs through the demands for a 'new international economic order'. Hence it is suggested that commodity markets need to be stabilised in order to avoid the excessive instability of the market and that private capital flows are an unsatisfactory means of bringing about a transfer of resources for the purpose of development. At the same time, it has been consistently claimed that the rules of the international economic order should not apply to the developing countries and, indeed, that the principle of discrimination is perfectly satisfactory, provided only that its application takes a form favourable to them. The Generalised System of Preferences enshrines this attitude to international trade. In fact, it is important to note that during the

54

Tokyo Round of multilateral trade negotiations, conducted under the auspices of the GATT in 1973-79, the developing countries became a lobby against tariff reductions, just because they would erode the benefits from these discriminatory arrangements.

Again, it is important to recognise that these views are deep-seated, having their counterparts in domestic economic policy. In most developing countries, it has become accepted dogma that government is responsible for development and, too, that both extensive intervention and comprehensive planning are essential in order to offset the presumed defects of the market. These attitudes are not merely intellectual; the power and influence of established elites depend on their continued acceptance. These same opinions have as their natural corollary the desire to plan and manage the world economy. But the relationship is deeper even than that. Since the domestic policies lead almost inevitably to economic failure, the existing international economic order becomes a convenient scapegoat; at the same time, the demand for 'something for nothing' from the developed countries offers an avenue of escape from the consequences of mistaken domestic policies. Unfortunately, however, this escape consists of attempting to impose on the world economy what has already failed at the national level.

Consequences of Developing-country Demands

The effect of the developing countries' philosophical assault on the international economic order itself is important. One result is to lead opinion makers in the developed countries to question whether the order can really be beneficial for them if so large a group of countries believes it harmful to their own interests. Some, who are both well-intentioned and confused, do not wish to support an order that they come to see as beneficial to themselves, but harmful to the truly needy. On the other hand, the defenders of particular interests in the developed countries argue that the developing countries are being allowed to devastate the industries of the developed world while protecting their own industries to the hilt. More generally, the insistence by the developing countries on their unique problems and need for differential treatment encourages an attitude of querulous benevolence on the part of the developed countries, giving special favours when the developing countries fail and imposing special obstacles when they succeed.

In all these ways, the protagonists of the positions of the developing countries, the Brandt Commission among them, have encouraged the undermining of faith in the liberal principles of the international economic order and the private enterprise that thrives within that order. Ultimately, the international economic order is probably not sustainable if a large group of countries continues to argue that the developed countries are obliged to preserve completely open markets towards them, in accordance with its liberal principles of the order, while denying both the need and, more important, the wisdom of reciprocating in any way.

NOTES AND REFERENCES

1.Adam Smith, *An Inquiry into the Nature and Causes of the Wealth of Nations* (London: Strahan and Cadell, 1776). A modern edition, edited by Edwin Cannan, has been published by the University of Chicago Press, Chicago and London, 1976.

2.Keynes, *The General Theory of Employment, Interest and Money* (London: Macmillan, 1936).

3.Hans-Heinrich Glismann, Hans Rodemer and Frank Wolter, *Zur Natur der Wachstumsschwache in der Bundesrepublik Deutschland: Eine empirische Analyse langer Zyklen wirtschaftlicher Entwicklung*, Kiel Discussion Paper No. 55 (Kiel: Institut für Weltwirtschaft an der Universität Kiel, 1978).

4.H. G. Johnson, Foreword to Geoffrey Denton, Seamus O'Cleireacain and Sally Ash, *Trade Effects of Public Subsidies to Private Enterprise* (London: Macmillan, for the Trade Policy Research Centre, 1975; and New York: St Martin's Press, 1975).

5.Tumlir, 'The Contribution of Economics to International Disorder', Second Harry G. Johnson Memorial Lecture, *The World Economy*, January 1981.

6.These issues have been discussed in four articles in *The World Economy:* Tumlir, 'Salvation Through Cartels? On the Revival of a Myth' (October 1978); Kurt Stockman, 'Contradictions Over Competition in the Leading Industrial Countries' (October 1978); Kent Jones, 'Forgetfulness of Things Past: Europe and the Steel Cartel' (May 1979); and René Joliet, 'Cartelisation, Dirigism and Crisis in the European Community' (January 1981).

7.A review of the modern forms of protection can be found in Bahram Nowzad, *The Rise of Protectionism* (Washington: IMF, 1978) and Melvyn Krauss, *The New Protectionism* (Oxford: Basil Blackwell, 1979).

An analysis of the market for protection appears in Helen Hughes and Jean Waelbroeck, 'Can Developing-country Exports Keep Growing in the 1980s?', *The World Economy*, June 1981.

8.Kerry Schott, *Industrial Innovation in the United Kingdom, Canada and the United States* (London, Washington and Montreal: British-North American Committee, 1981).

9.For a full discussion of these points, see Giersch, 'Neglected Aspects of Inflation in the World Economy', *Public Finance*, The Hague, Vol. 28, No. 2, 1973, and Tumlir, 'Economics, Economic Policy and Inflation', *The Banker*, London, October 1979.

10.Staffan Burenstam-Linder, 'How to Avoid a New International Economic Disorder', *The World Economy*, November 1980.

11.Brandt Report, *op. cit.*, p. 32.

CHAPTER FIVE

Brandt Report on the Need for Increased Official Aid

THE BRANDT Report has been carefully assessed in various publications[1] and therefore it is not the intention to examine it in detail here. Of the main themes, though, two are considered elsewhere in this report. The contention that market forces necessarily make for inequality has been discussed immediately above. The search for 'mutual interests' between developed and developing countries will be dealt with in the next chapter. In this chapter will be considered the advocacy of a substantial increase in the transfer of resources as a prerequisite for development and the advocacy, too, of related suggestions for the reform of the international institutions.

TRANSFERS FOR DEVELOPMENT

Before analysing transfers of resources, however, there is a general issue to be addressed, namely, the notion that such transfers are owed to developing countries because of the exploitation of these countries during the Western colonial period.

Myths of Western Colonialism

There are aspects of the Western colonial period, such as the slave trade and instances of repression of native peoples, that were indefensible. But the different assessments of Western colonialism have confused discussion of the issues that are relevant today to economic development in the Third World and especially to the case for transfers of resources from developed to developing countries.

Backward economic conditions in some former colonial territories are regularly paraded as being the result of 'exploitation'—inferring, in this context, the draining away of wealth by the occupying powers. The implication is that if left to their own devices these countries would have developed standards of living comparable with those of Western countries.[2] The West, generally, is accused of having become rich by making the poor poorer. It is thus thought, or said, by many that the West should feel guilty for poverty in the Third World and consequently should be prepared to transfer resources back to less well-off countries as reparations, so to speak, for economic wrongs purportedly perpetrated at some time in the past.

If the 'exploitation' theory were valid there would be many anomalies to explain away. The countries that had colonies should be the ones to have enjoyed the highest standards of living, but Canada, Sweden and Switzerland have had very high standards of living without ever having been colonial powers. Afghanistan, which had never been occupied until the recent Soviet invasion, has a relatively low standard of living that cannot be attributed to colonial exploitation. Hong Kong, still a colony, has one of the highest standards of living in East Asia. If exploitation, the draining away of wealth, had been the order of the day in the period of Western colonialism, the 'occupied' territories would have been poorer when the colonial rulers left than when they arrived. But, in looking at the Third World, this is manifestly untrue in Africa and Asia.

To take an example, Malaysia is one of the more prosperous of the developing countries, having become independent of the United Kingdom in 1957. Many factors have contributed to her economic growth, but three of her main export crops, namely rubber, palm oil and cocoa, are not indigenous to the country. The rubber seeds came from Brazil, via Kew Gardens in London and the Botanical Gardens in Singapore, while the oil palms came from West Africa and the cocoa came from both West Africa and Trinidad. Their transposition to Malaya and subsequent development were due to investment decisions by companies and smallholders of many nationalities. The clearing of jungle and the establishment of cash crops suitable to the local climate and soil can only be described as the creation of a new source of wealth. To describe developments of this kind as draining wealth from a country is to sacrifice intellectual probity to fantasy.

The Scope of the Problem

The analysis which follows concentrates on official transfer of resources to developing countries, whether through bilateral or multilateral institutions, that depend in the end on the taxation of the citizens of developed countries. Programmes that are funded from the government budgets of developed countries as well as from the proposals for automatic transfers are covered. Private lending motivated by profit is excluded. The World Bank's lending of funds borrowed from commercial sources—a borderline case—may be regarded as 'official' for present purposes. The analysis is not concerned with indirect transfers of resources through international commodity arrangements, which pose other issues.

Discussion of the Brandt Commission's views on official development assistance has been coloured by the Commission's use of the term 'massive transfers' of resources which would seem to imply transfers on a considerably larger scale than hitherto. From the substance of its recommendations, however, the Brandt Commission is chiefly concerned with the achievement by the developed countries of an aid target by 1985 of 0.7 per cent of GNP, the level urged by the Pearson Commission back in 1969.

In considering the proposed increase in the transfer of

official resources from the industrialised to the developing countries, two questions can be raised. First, what is the justification for making official transfers? And, secondly, what is their economic value? These questions are related —especially for those whose faith in transfers of resources is based on utilitarian considerations. They are nevertheless distinct. Thus, for those who argue that the rich have a general moral obligation to help the poor, the efficacy of official development assistance is more or less irrelevant. But the benefits of transfers of resources is the decisive issue for most people, those who do not believe that such transfers are a moral imperative, independent of consequences.

Direct Role of Resource Transfers

Earlier, in Chapter 2, it was argued that large transfers of resources, whether made on concessional terms or not, were neither a necessary nor a sufficient condition for economic development. What is crucial are the talents and skills of the population and the economic institutions and policies which allow and encourage such talents and skills to produce results.

If all other factors determining development are held constant, transfers of resources work by raising permitted levels of expenditure in the recipient country or countries. The more concessional the terms, the more expenditure is raised over the long term, for the smaller is the proportion of the initial transfer that has to be repaid. In any given period, there comes a limit beyond which further investment ceases to be fruitful, usually because the lack of administrative capacity to execute, or entrepreneurial ability to identify, further investment opportunities. Beyond this point transfers of resources are best used to support consumption.

It follows that it is countries with the most developed human resources, and which also pursue policies that guide investment in efficient directions, which are able to exploit transfers of resources most successfully. If such countries are short of physical infrastructure, perhaps because of war, returns will be particularly high. The success of the Marshall Plan in Europe and the reconstruction of Japan after World War II, frequently listed as cases *par excellence* of a fruitful transfer of resources on the grand scale, depended on existing attitudes and aptitudes combined with a lack of physical capital.[3] In spite of massive destruction, Germany and Japan still retained the managerial and financial expertise necessary to run a developed economy, while both countries had a labour force that was literate and skilled. The problem with which the Marshall Plan was designed to cope was essentially one of restoration and there is thus no analogy with conditions in the developing countries today.

Taiwan and South Korea shared some of the same characteristics of Germany and Japan after World War II, especially the favourable attitudes of their people and the need, as well, to make good the losses of war. Whilst transfers of resources unquestionably helped to establish infrastructure for development, the experience of these countries, however, confirms the primacy of policy. Thus their 'miracle' growth in the 1960s followed a move to export-oriented policies, which itself occurred when cheap transfers were declining. In a short period of time, Taiwan became a net creditor, while South Korea borrowed increasingly on commercial terms.[4]

In sum, transfers of resources on their own can undoubtedly have a positive effect as has been indicated by detailed studies of a number of developing countries, but their value is likely to be greatest to those likely to do quite well even without them. In other cases, returns on investments can fall to negligible levels quite rapidly as transfers increase; and the benefits of transfers are likely to consist largely of increases in consumption which might themselves be desirable in certain circumstances.

Indirect Effects of Resource Transfers

It is because of the primacy of what lies within a society rather than what can be obtained from outside that the subject of transfers of resources is so controversial. The reason is that all the other factors cannot be held constant —as was assumed above. Among other things, the attitudes of the people, the institutional framework and economic policy might be affected by large transfers. The controversy, then, is about whether these indirect effects will be negative, positive or neutral.

The case for the positive impact of transfers of resources (beyond the benefit of the transfers themselves) depends on the impact on economic policy and, too, on knowledge and skill more generally. Transfers can, and do, come with strings attached. They also frequently come wrapped up with extensive advice and technical assistance. It can be argued that transfers in these forms have positive effects beyond those of the resources themselves.[5]

One of the classic examples of transfers of resources 'buying' policy improvement is the Marshall Plan which brought about European economic liberalisation.[6] The IMF is constantly trying to bring about the same result. The World Bank and other development agencies are also engaged in dispensing advice and technical assistance along with their project aid.

Since appropriate policies are a necessary condition for the productive investment of large transfers of resources, using them as a lever for bringing about changes in policy seems appropriate, but there are problems.[7] First, this kind of transfer tends to infringe on a country's sovereignty; and infringement of sovereignty is objectionable to many of those convinced of the moral justification for transfers from rich to poor countries. Secondly, external advisers can be wrong. Thirdly, there can be tension between the aim of inducing policy change and that of giving large transfers, since the latter can obviate the need for the former. Fourthly, a government can undermine a policy package of whose wisdom it is itself unconvinced. Finally, the constraints that limit the ability to spend sums productively can also limit the ability to absorb advice. In short, while transfers can have positive indirect effects, the conditions under which they will are not universal.

By way of contrast, critics of official development assistance suggest that the deleterious effects on polity and policy far exceed the direct benefits of transfers. Policy may deteriorate because of excessive government control over the resources transferred, because of insistence by donors on central planning, because of the encouragement of large resource gaps in the balance of payments, or because of relaxation of pressure to improve policy. The polity itself may be adversely affected if the sense that there is a relation between effort and reward diminishes or, more seriously, if an influx of wealth undermines the social fabric and political stability. This last is more likely if the wealth arrives from outside rather than being generated within the society.[8]

The sudden rise in the price of oil after 1973 was in effect a large unconditional transfer of resources from oil-importing to oil-exporting countries. The problems the oil-exporting countries have faced, however, in using these resources wisely within their countries indicate that such a large transfer is very far from a panacea. The collapse of Iran suggests that the social upheavals generated by rapid and unbalanced change created by increased resources from outside can be devastating.

It is not easy to make any general statement about whether positive or negative indirect effects will predominate—although the essential condition for the former is wise domestic policies. For all but enormous transfers of resources, the indirect effects are likely to be modest, whatever their direction. Thus the direct effects, which are positive, may be expected to predominate. The suggestion that, as a general proposition, aid should reach 0.7 per cent of GNP by 1985 could therefore be a sensible target, especially if the aid were accompanied by the kind of conditionality and control that made it more likely that the resources would be used productively. At the same time one should not expect miracles. It would, for instance, be a bold forecaster who would suggest that Britain will be turned by wealth even as large as that created by North Sea oil into another Japan or Germany. Transfers of resources are largely a marginal issue emphasised by those who do not accept the central role of society itself in generating change.

Resource Transfers and the Poor

Unfortunately, the conditions for using resources from outside effectively can sometimes conflict with the chief reason for transferring those resources, namely the extreme poverty of many citizens of developing countries. With a few exceptions, very undeveloped countries with large concentrations of poor people need very careful super-vision in the use of resources; and, furthermore, there is the possibility of negative indirect effects. This last would be especially true if the transfers were to be spent largely in bolstering consumption (as a kind of welfare benefit) because of an inability to expand investment adequately. There do exist dangers in reducing entire societies to the status of welfare dependents—as has occurred with refugees in some parts of the world. Criticism of the effects of food aid gives only a shadow of the controversies such transfers can create.[9]

Not all countries with large concentrations of poor face administrative problems in using substantial additional resources effectively. India, for example, has extensive administrative capacity, as do countries in Latin America, like Brazil, with extremely unequal income distribution. The problem here can be either inefficient overall economic policy, as in India,[10] or a social structure biased to some extent against equitable sharing of the fruits of development, as in Brazil.[11] In cases like these transfers will help the poor substantially only if policies are first changed and this should be a priority for donors.

Uses of Resource Transfers

It is difficult to argue that transfers of resources on their own can provide solutions to the problems of poor countries or poor peoples (which are by no means identical). The conditions under which such transfers will be useful are not universal. Moreover, what will be required will often amount to intervention in the internal policies of countries. Indeed, it is difficult to see how the developed countries can be expected to assume responsibility for development in the developing countries if they are to be deprived of any power to influence their policies.

It is also important to note that reasonably successful countries have increasing access to resource transfers on commercial terms from private capital markets. It is only poor or ill-managed countries that are largely precluded from these markets. This development further limits the number of cases in which transfers of resources from official sources are vital.

What, then, should be the main use of such transfers? There seem to be four distinct cases.

The first is that of a country which needs to change the direction of policy and wants to do so, but is experiencing severe balance-of-payments difficulties and is lacking credit worthiness. These legacies of past errors can be remedied by outside support if policy change is in the right direction. Turkey is an important apparent example of such assistance. Policy change to help development of productive activity by poorer people and, more generally to help the poor participate more fully, may also be 'bought' by external transfers. It should be emphasised that these interventions are unlikely to succeed if the governments concerned do not want them to do so.

A second case is that of the least developed countries that do not have the capacity to commence projects that will pay back commercial debt. For such countries, external assistance may accelerate the slow process of building up essential infrastructure for development and support the consumption levels of the people. While this can be a useful role for assistance, the adverse effects of large-scale aid need to be carefully watched. Tanzania is a salient case of an extensively aided country that has performed poorly.[12]

A third case is where countries are dependent on export revenue from one or a few commodities and are therefore liable to suffer a serious shortfall in export revenue if the prices of those commodities should fall. Provision is made for these eventualities in the IMF's compensatory financing facility and in the 'Stabex' arrangement under the Lomé Convention between the European Community and some sixty developing countries in Africa, the Caribbean and the Pacific (certain former colonies of Community countries).

A fourth case is international relief to offset the effects on poor countries of famines, war and other calamities.

These four possible uses for official assistance necessitate supervision and a discriminating and careful approach. Transfers of resources without strings and without limit, even if politically possible, could do almost as much damage as good.

Resource Transfers and Recycling

There is the special problem of managing a world with large and apparently permanent current-account surpluses in some countries.[13] It can be argued that the goals of industrialised countries and many oil exporters make it necessary for developing countries to run large current-account deficits. If the latter cannot be financed, equilibrium in the global balance of payments may be brought about at a low level of economic activity. Furthermore, some countries that lack creditworthiness may be forced to curtail real expenditures sharply even if overall equilibrium is achieved at generally high levels of economic activity.

Transfers of resources to maintain levels of economic activity, or to support prior levels of real expenditure, do not bear the same risks as those discussed more generally above. At the same time, the case for transfers, which can only be a short- to medium-term one, is separate from that for substantial long-term transfers from developed to developing countries. It is likely in fact that, as has been recognised by the IMF and the World Bank, some official assistance with the recycling process is useful as a supplement to the dominant role of the private financial institutions in recycling to the larger and more successful developing countries some of the current-account surpluses accruing to the oil-exporting countries. Here, too, the need for discretion must be acknowledged, for adjustment to the terms-of-trade change will be required in due course.

Verdict on Transfers of Resources

Transfers of resources from official sources to developing countries cannot be generally condemned or generally endorsed. In certain circumstances their efficacy is undoubted. Making transfers truly productive, however, is not only difficult but likely to involve conditionality, which is deemed objectionable by many protagonists of such transfers. Even if the target of 0.7 per cent of the GNP of developed countries was achieved and that aid concentrated on the poorest countries it would be wrong to expect miraculous changes. The dangers of emphasis on transfers lie not so much in any harmful effects as in legitimising a myth. Development does not drop like manna from heaven. It is generated from within society. Transfers of resources can be the hand-maiden, but not the engine, of growth. In this respect, it can be argued that the Brandt Report, in emphasising so whole-heartedly the virtues of resource transfers, has missed the basic development issue.

Effects on Developed Countries

It has been argued by some, including the Brandt Commission, that, apart from their effect on the recipients, substantial transfers of resources would also be in the narrow self-interest of the donor countries since this would assist in pulling them out of recession. Basic to the argument is the Commission's belief that the low rates of growth, both currently and in the 1970s, were the result of a shortfall in aggregate demand. This is a view which is coming under increasing challenge; but even if it were true, changes in domestic policy would achieve the same end and in present circumstances of unemployment could well prove politically more attractive. Eradication of poverty and slum clearance are not the preserve of developing countries alone. On the other hand, insofar as inflation in the developed countries has been caused by an excess of demand, any massive transfer of funds would only compound the problem.

INTERNATIONAL INSTITUTIONS

The Brandt Report had a great deal to say about the role of international, or inter-governmental, institutions in bringing about the desired massive transfer of resources. It also recommended the creation of new institutions and mechanisms. For a long time, in fact, the Group of 77 has been pressing for a larger voice in international institutions, particularly in the financial ones. The demands, essentially, are four: more money, less strings, more control and more institutions. Yet it is far from clear that these goals are severally desirable or collectively feasible.

69

Problems with Developing-country Demands

The inappropriateness of some of the demands follows from what has already been said. Official transfers of resources without strings are unlikely to achieve much. Countries that have the skills and the policies to use them effectively have ready access to the private capital markets, which are certain to continue to transfer much larger resources than the official multilateral donors—namely the World Bank, the regional development banks *et cetera*. Countries that lack those skills and policies might waste the money, especially if it comes without the strings that are so much resented. Throwing money at the development problem is almost bound to be a disappointing exercise. It is understandable that the leaders of the developing countries demand transfers without strings. But it is just those countries that most resent the conditions imposed that are likely, because of their inappropriate policies, to waste transfers that come without them.

When it comes to participation in the decision-making process of the inter-governmental institutions, the Group of 77 has become rather influential in the Interim Committee of the IMF, established to oversee the reform of the international monetary system, and the Development Committee of the IMF and the World Bank, established as a forum for the discussion of development issues. If matters are pushed to a vote, the Group of 77 can usually rely on support from outside its ranks to achieve a majority. On the whole, though, the executive bodies of the two institutions work by consensus, which is to say that the demands of the Group of 77 for increased voting power are only of limited relevance. In the GATT, voting strengths are not weighted, each country having one vote, but there are limits to what can be pushed to a vote in an institutional framework in which issues have to be settled by consultation and negotiation. Greater participation and control in decision making does not necessarily yield greater benefits. The overwhelming interest of developing countries in the international system of trade and payments is that the major developed countries maintain the convertibility of their currencies and adhere to liberal trade policies, preferably with exchange-rate stability and with little inflation; the participation in decision making of countries with marginal interests (and a tendency to demand aid and preferential treatment) can serve to thwart agreement on the complex issues entailed.

The desire to create new institutions, whenever there is a new problem, is also misconceived. There are already a very large number of organisations, both inside and outside the United Nations system, concerned with the problems of development. It would be difficult to think of any topic, especially within the economic sphere, which is not the concern of one or other of them and usually of more than one.

In recent years a substantial effort has been devoted within the United Nations itself to bring some order and system into this situation and to make sure that the very considerable amounts of money that are spent by these organisations, both in the execution of the tasks assigned to them and on their administration, are used properly and efficiently. Even so, it seems to have become the practice to establish a new organisation when a particular problem is isolated for consideration; and this is in face of the fact that already the structure of international organisation is almost certainly overblown.

Quite apart from cost, the call on available qualified manpower draws into the international institutions many of the very people whose talents and abilities are in short supply in their home countries. And the record of the achievements of most of the institutions is, at best, very mixed. Of course the picture varies. Valuable work is done by some of the specialised agencies, especially the more technical bodies, such as the International Telecommunications Union. No one who is familiar with the way that the whole machine works, however, would deny that it is in general cumbersome and inefficient, with many purely technical problems becoming clouded in inter-governmental debate by the complications of international political controversy; and the examination of possible solutions to issues is frequently distorted by irrelevant considerations.

Aside from the wisdom of the individual demands— more money, less strings, more control and more institutions—there must be doubt about whether they can all be had together. Who will lend money to a bank that is controlled by its debtors? Yet this remarkable demand is made of the World Bank. It is evident that the success this institution has had in attracting private money on a large scale has resulted from the perception that it follows prudent policies and demands appropriate performance from its clients. The aim of increasing the transfer of resources through such institutions, evidenced in the Brandt Report, is incompatible with the desire to reduce 'conditionality' and dilute the control of the creditors. This would perhaps be unimportant if the idea, advanced by the Brandt Commission, of taxation for development were ever to be successful, but this proposal appears no more than a fantasy.

Equally puzzling is the failure to recognise that the main institutions, the IMF and the World Bank (especially the former), play an important role as catalysts of private capital flows. The knowledge that there exist institutions with the authority to give policy advice to countries in difficulties is an important guarantee to private lenders. If the IMF did not exist it would probably have to be invented. Viewing the institutions simply in terms of the sums they transfer themselves is to misunderstand the role that they now play in the larger picture.

Indeed, it can be argued that both the IMF and World Bank have already gone much too far towards transferring

72

resources with minimal strings and have, therefore, diluted their unique role as watchdogs over macro-economic and long-term development policy, respectively. Access to IMF funds has been expanded and borrowing periods extended through the establishment of new facilities: the buffer-stock financing facility (1970), to assist countries with balance-of-payments deficits to finance contributions to buffer stocks set up under international commodity agreements; the extend fund facility (1974), to provide longer term financing for members with structural balance-of-payments problems; the oil facility (1975-76), which provided assistance for countries with oil-induced balance-of-payments deficits; the oil-facility interest-subsidy account, to subsidise interest costs on purchases from the oil facility by the 'most seriously affected' developing countries; the liberalisation of the compensatory financing facility (1975), to assist developing countries whose balance of payments have been affected by a shortfall in export earnings due to a fall in commodity prices; the supplementary financing facility (1979), to assist developing countries whose financing needs are large in proportion to their IMF quotas; the further liberalisation of the compensatory financing facility (1979); the establishment of an interest subsidy account (1980), to subsidise the cost of drawings on the supplementary financing facility by low-income countries; and a food financing facility (1981).

In addition, the 'conditionality' of drawings on the IMF have been greatly relaxed and IMF funds, as well as World Bank funds, have been expanding. At the end of 1980, all outstanding IMF commitments were to developing countries, Africa accounting for half. In other words, the IMF has become, for all intents and purposes, an institution providing balance-of-payments aid to developing countries for ever increasing periods. And repayment of IMF loans, when they become due, seems to be an increasingly remote possibility.

Although the demands made by the developing countries and their spokesmen are largely irrelevant, there are major issues facing the international institutions, especially for the World Bank and the IMF. In particular, three events of the 1970s have changed their environment fundamentally. The first was the collapse in 1971 of the system of fixed rates of exchange between the major currencies, which deprived the IMF of its historic purpose. The second was the rapid growth of lending by private financial institutions, especially the commercial banks, to the developing countries. And the third was the emergence of higher oil prices and the permanent current-account surpluses of some oil-exporting countries. This last change provided the IMF with a new role in recycling 'petro-dollars' and led the World Bank to its current interest in lending for 'structural adjustment'. In consequence, the respective roles of these institutions have become blurred; and have increasingly overlapped with the role of the private capital market.

These confusions are to some extent inevitable. Complete tidiness is too much to expect and, in any case, institutions must be permitted enough flexibility to adapt to changing circumstances. Even so, the central roles of the institutions must not be forgotten, since they remain immensely important. In the case of the IMF, that role is to remain as a watchdog over the macro-economic policies of their clients and as an impartial source of advice. In the case of the World Bank, it is to provide counsel on long-term development policy and, too, to finance the sorts of projects for which private finance is unlikely to be available in adequate quantity. It is not sensible for either institution to attempt to become, at one extreme, just another bank or, at another extreme, a writer of blank cheques for developing countries. What is important in the maintenance of a stable international economic order is the recognition that governments should

74

not have unlimited freedom of action. As with the GATT, the curtailment of the sovereignty of individual nations by institutions like the IMF and the World Bank is, and was always intended to be, in the interests of all.

NOTES AND REFERENCES

1. See, for example, P. D. Henderson, 'Survival, Development and the Report of the Brandt Commission', *The World Economy*, June 1980; and Dudley Seers, 'North-South: Muddling Morality and Mutuality', *Third World Quarterly*, London, October 1980.

2. For example, in Gunnar Myrdal, *The Equality Issue in World Development* (Stockholm: Swedish Academy of Sciences, 1975), it is asserted that the old 'colonial empires' neglected or possibly exploited their less developed regions, which 'stagnated in poverty'.

3. For a discussion of the Marshall Plan, its pre-conditions and consequences, see D. H. Aldcroft, *The European Economy* (London: Croom Helm, 1978); William Diebold, *Trade and Payments in Western Europe: Study in Economic Co-operation 1947-51* (New York: Harper, for the Council on Foreign Relations, 1952); and M. M. Postan, *An Economic History of Western Europe* (London: Methuen, 1967).

4. There exists an enormous literature on the growth of Taiwan and South Korea. The most interesting discussion of their comparative performance and of the respective roles of aid, human and natural resources and policies is contained in Little, 'An Economic Reconnaissance', in Walter Galenson (ed.), *Economic Growth and Structural Change in Taiwan: the Postwar Experience of the Republic of China* (Ithaca: Cornell University Press, 1979), Ch. 7, pp. 448-507. In this paper, the experience of Hong Kong, Japan and Singapore is also discussed. Professor Little concludes on Taiwan that 'apart from the creation of a virtual free trade regime for exports, the conservative government budgeting, high interests rates and a free labour market—a set of features that, in the past, many development economists would have held to be a certain recipe for stagnation and inequality—it is hard to find any good explanation for the sustained industrial boom of 1963-1973' (*ibid.*, p. 480).

In an important book on South Korea, Charles Frank Jr, Kwang Suk Kim and Larry E. Westphal state that special factors including aid 'are not sufficient in themselves to explain the success of the South Korean economy. Economic policies made an important contribution: tax and government expenditure reforms, the interest-rate reforms, the exchange-rate reforms and the general emphasis on export promotion and reliance on international prices were some of the most critical.' See Frank, Kim and Westphal, *Foreign Trade Regimes and Economic Development: South Korea* (New York and London: Columbia University Press, for the National Bureau of Economic Research, 1975), p. 243. Furthermore, as the authors note, '... the periods of high levels of foreign aid are not coterminous with the periods of most rapid growth' (*ibid.*, p. 241).

5.One of the most thorough discussions of the benefits of aid is contained in the Pearson Report, *op. cit.*

6.This aspect of the Marshall Plan is commented upon in Tumlir, 'The Contribution of Economics to International Disorder', *loc. cit.*, pp. 397-8.

7.An argument for using aid as a lever for policy change is contained in Anne O. Krueger, 'Loans to Assist the Transition to Outward-looking Policies', *The World Economy*, September 1981.

8.P. T. Bauer, *Equality, the Third World and Economic Delusion* (London: Weidenfeld & Nicolson, 1981), pp. 103-9.

9.Paul Isenman and H. W. Singer discuss the effects of food aid, but come to the conclusion that the disincentive effects, at least of quantities offered in the past, did not outweigh their other benefits. See Isenman and Singer, 'Food Aid: Disincentive Effects and their Policy Implications', *Economic Development and Cultural Change*, Chicago, January 1977. The main example used in this paper is India. It can, however, be argued against the authors that major and successful changes in India's policies followed the Government's perception that massive food aid was a thing of the past. This line of reasoning is highly speculative.

10.The effects of Indian policies on employment generation and poverty are discussed in J. W. Mellor, *The New Economics of Growth* (Ithaca: Cornell University Press, 1976). On India's basic development policies, see Bhagwati and Padma Desai, *India: Planning for Industrialisation—Industrialisation and Trade Policies since 1951* (London, New York and Bombay: Oxford University Press, for the Organisation for Economic Cooperation and Development, 1970). For an interesting discussion of the harmful effects of India's policies on industrial employment, see Ranadev Banerji and James Riedel, 'Industrial Employment Expansion Under Alternative Trade Strategies: Case of India and Taiwan: 1950-70', *Journal of Development Economics*, Amsterdam, December 1980.

11.Edmar L. Bacha and Lance Taylor argue that 'labour surplus conditions and repressive labour policies help explain why Brazilian workers near the median of the size distribution benefitted little if any from economic growth in the 1960s'. (The persistence of labour-surplus conditions may be explained in part by a bias towards capital-intensive development.) See Bacha and Taylor, 'Brazilian Income Distribution in the 1960s: "Facts", Model Results and the Controversy', in Taylor, Bacha, Eliana A. Cardoso and Frank J. Lysy, *Models of Growth and Distribution for Brazil* (New York: Oxford University Press, for the World Bank, 1980), p. 329.

12.A discussion of Tanzania's development policies, contrasted with those of more market-oriented African countries like Kenya, is contained in Shankar N. Acharya, 'Perspectives and Problems of Development in Low-income, Sub-Saharan Africa', and Acharya and Bruce Johnston (eds), *Two Studies of Development in Sub-Saharan Africa*, World Bank Staff Working Paper No. 300 (Washington: World Bank, 1978).

13.These issues are assessed in Graeme S. Dorrance, 'Capital for Development', a paper prepared for the Study Group.

CHAPTER SIX

Conclusions on a Strategy for Growth

THE PURPOSE of this report has been to highlight for public discussion the role of private enterprise in the process of development and economic growth. In seeking to clarify this role the discussion of private enterprise has necessarily been set in the context of the principles of economic development in an open world economy. The rapid integration of the world economy, making for growing interdependence between national economies, and the demands for a 'new international economic order' required this.

Before conclusions are drawn about a strategy for growth, it might be useful to recall the main thrust of the argument. The report has stressed that the tendency, over the last decade and a half at least, to discount the importance of market forces in the process of economic growth has meant that not enough attention has been paid by governments to the principles on which nations can live amicably together in peace and prosperity. Reliance on markets necessarily involves private enterprise and, what is more, it underlies the international economic order that was instituted after World War II, contributing significantly to the restoration of growth and prosperity in the 1950s and 1960s.

There has recently been a tendency to replace the dynamic concept of economic activity by a zero-sum mentality, by a philosophy which ignores what the future can offer and concentrates on what the past has already delivered. It has also been stressed therefore that economic development is a positive-sum game in which the opportunities for growth expand with the size of the market.

Two Distinct Foci of Concern

Two distinct foci of concern have been addressed: the dissatisfaction of the developing countries with the international economic order which is perceived by many to work in the interests of developed countries; and the economic problems of the developed countries which are affecting their relations not only with each other but also with the developing countries. The link between the two concerns can be found in the impairment of the market process which has been steadily worsening since the 1960s.

Government intervention in the market process has created cumulative difficulties: nationally, through the spread of public assistance from one sector of industry to another; and internationally, through the growth of friction between governments as foreign scapegoats are sought for failures in domestic policies.

Thus, in the broadest terms, for these difficulties to be resolved it is necessary to 'de-politicise' national economies and the world economy as far as possible—by returning to market principles. A conscious effort has to be made to render policies as general as possible by minimising discrimination between persons, firms, industries and countries. This is now coming to be increasingly recognised by national governments and international organisations.[1] By mid-1981 the seventh Economic Summit meeting in Ottawa, the Bank for International Settlements (BIS), the IMF, the OECD and GATT had all drawn attention to the consequences of government intervention and asserted the importance of the market process.[2]

Thus the proposals of the Brandt Report, reflecting the determination of the Group of 77 to achieve the 'politicisation' of the economic problem of development, represent a return to the thinking which was responsible for the current *impasse*. The attack of the Group of 77 on the liberal principles of the international system of trade and payments has been mistaken, especially the distrust of the market process and private enterprise as the engine of wealth creation and, too, the inclination to believe that external support and international institutions can be substitutes for sound domestic policies. It is true, however, that the trends of trade, industrial and labour policies in North America and Western Europe lend substance to complaints about protectionism.

In brief, the North-South dialogue should not be about a 'new' international economic order; it should be about how to make more effective the liberal principles of the present international economic order within which, in spite of all the difficulties, an increasing number of developing countries are making noticeable progress.

Repair of the International Economic Order

All countries share responsibility for achieving solutions to the problems of the international economic order. But the bulk of international transactions, in both trade and finance, occur among a comparatively small number of developed countries. It is these countries which must bear the brunt. If they can achieve stable institutional arrangements among themselves, the extension of these arrangements on a non-discriminatory basis to the many smaller countries means that there is an 'international order', one based on market principles.

The 'crisis' in the international economic order has to be viewed in two complementary parts: financial and trade. At present, there is much anxiety about the stability of the international financial system and, with all the calls for reform of the rules, about the stability of the international trading system. What is to be done?

Policies of Developed Countries

In relation to the developed countries there are three sets of issues to be confronted.

First, without domestic price stability, the price mechanism cannot work effectively. Inflation is essentially a domestic problem, the product of domestic policies, and can only be stopped by domestic actions. Stopping inflation must be the top priority of governments if their economies are to return to the path of sustained growth. For that it will be necessary to make an impact on people's expectations of what their government can and will do. Expectations formed over a period of twenty years, however, are not easily changed.

On the international implications of inflation, societies trying to live with other than minimal inflation soon fall to internal conflicts; national governments accordingly become preoccupied with maintaining internal cohesion and cannot devote enough attention to international cooperation. Current tensions over rates of interest show how difficult it is to maintain good relations between countries in a world in which rates of inflation differ widely from country to country with consequential effects on exchange-rate fluctuation.

Second, there is anxiety about the stability and security of the international financial system, stemming mainly from the heavy borrowing by developing countries from private financial institutions. The owners and guarantors of these institutions are in the largest developed countries which at the same time represent the main markets for the exports of the debtor countries. It therefore follows that the developed countries will be contributing to the discharge of their main responsibility for international financial stability if, through adherence to liberal trade policies, they help these debtor countries to earn means of repayment.

Third, the anxiety about the stability of the international trading system arises from the growth of government intervention since the mid-1960s, with tariffs and import quotas being replaced as the instruments of protection by public subsidies of various kinds, other non-tariff measures, 'voluntary' export restraints and sectoral agreements of a cartel character. Many of the instruments of 'neo-protectionism' have only recently been made subject to codes of conduct within the GATT framework.

The principle of non-discrimination is the only safeguard that a country's share in another country's market remains an acquired right, challengeable only by more efficient producers, but secured from government interference. In this way the strict application of most-favoured-nation treatment offers security not only to foreign exporters but also to the government of the importing country. If governments intrude further into the business of determining market shares, as they have done most conspicuously with the Multi-fibre Arrangement covering trade in textiles and clothing (but also with footwear, steel, motor vehicles, consumer electronics *et cetera*), it will become more and more difficult for them to coexist peacefully.

Since the early 1970s, the governments of the major trading countries have reasserted their commitment to the principles and rules of the GATT system of international trade. But they have felt obliged to make concessions here and there, allowing exceptions to the rule, hoping thereby to maintain the integrity of the rules as a whole. Merely verbal reaffirmations of GATT principles and rules are therefore no longer enough. Governments should begin repudiating the precedents that have permitted deviations from GATT principles and rules. The repudiation of precedents such as the Multi-fibre Arrangement would not only be significant in itself but also be significant as a signal to non-protected industries.

There is no denying the political problems in such a

course for the governments of developed countries. But electorates need to be properly informed of the costs and benefits of different courses of action. This is a matter of leadership and of fulfilling the information function of government.

Policies of Developing Countries

In relation to the developing countries there are two sets of issues.

First, in order to promote the efficient allocation of domestic resources, developing countries need to liberalise restrictions and controls in their domestic policies. Policies for promoting economic development should be as non-discriminatory as possible as between persons, firms and industries. While planned economies and market economies have succeeded in developing, the latter have generally out-performed the former. The role of policy choice and private entrepreneurship is illuminated by comparisons between countries with different policies and institutions, but almost identical human resources, as with East and West Germany, in Europe, and North and South Korea, in Asia. Those countries where growth has been fast have created the conditions which have attracted private investment, whether domestic or foreign, and have afforded scope for the successful operation of private enterprise.

Second, it has been noted that the most successful developing countries have pursued export-oriented policies and this requires that in their own interests they dismantle many restrictions on imports. Trade liberalisation would assist the efficient allocation of domestic resources (and it would also provide opportunities in their markets for other developing countries, including the least developed ones, for in recent years intra-Third World trade has been expanding rapidly).

The willingness to adopt outward-looking strategies for development, based on export-oriented policies, depends on the continuance of liberal trade policies in the developed countries.

Hence the developing countries have much to lose from an increase in economic nationalism. As their weight in the world economy has increased, so too has their interest in, and their responsibility for, a liberal international economic order. They have a stake in the observance of liberal trade rules and in the further liberalisation of trade. Their participation in both should therefore be undertaken as soon as possible. For the more successful developing countries the time for that has come.

TRANSFERS OF RESOURCES

Considerable attention has been paid in the report to the demands of the developing countries for substantial transfers of resources from the developed countries. Historically, large transfers, whether conditional or not, have been neither a necessary nor a sufficient condition for economic development. There are, however, cases where such transfers can be useful. Where countries need to change the direction of policy, but are experiencing some balance-of-payments difficulties and lack credit-worthiness, these legacies of past errors can be remedied by outside support if policy change is in the right direction. In the least developed countries that have limited capacity to commence projects which will pay back commercial debts, external assistance may accelerate the slow process of building up essential infrastructure for development and support low consumption levels. When countries dependent on export revenue from one or a few commodities suffer a serious shortfall in earnings through falling prices, compensatory financing may be desirable. But these uses of official assistance necessitate a discriminating and careful approach. Achieving an aid target of 0.7 per cent of the GNP of developed countries and concentrating aid on the poorest countries could have a positive effect, especially if the aid were accompanied by the kind of conditionality that makes it more likely that the resources will be used productively.

The IMF and the World Bank have their part to play in the transfer of resources and must be permitted enough flexibility to adapt to changing circumstances. But in the process, the central role of these institutions must not be forgotten. In the case of the IMF, that role is to remain as a watchdog over the short-term economic policies of their clients and as an impartial source of advice. In the case of the World Bank, it is to provide counsel on long-term development policy and to finance the sort of projects for which private finance is unlikely to be available in adequate quantity. Neither institution should be allowed to become either just another bank or a provider of excessively easy money for developing countries.

QUESTION OF 'MUTUAL INTERESTS'

As remarked in the Brandt Report, the North-South dialogue has suffered from the atmosphere in which it is being conducted, for it has been proceeding in terms of 'demands' by the South and 'concessions' from the North. The Brandt Commission claims to break new ground by basing its recommendations on the 'mutual interests' of the North and the South. But beneath the surface of conciliatory phraseology, the adversary conception is clear, being inherent in 'conducting development' by regulation, redistribution of resources and constant negotiation.

As regards the Brandt Commission's identification of mutual interests, its contention that, quite apart from the affect on the developing countries, substantial transfers of resources would be in the interest of the developed countries also as a means of lifting the recession, has been challenged earlier in this report. Nevertheless, although many would differ with the Brandt Commission on where mutual interests might be found, all would share its view that solutions to North-South problems must be sought on that basis.

At present, the developed countries are experiencing serious economic difficulties, which means that development assistance for the countries of the Third World presents domestic political problems. Even so, there are manifold opportunities for mutually profitable transfers of resources through foreign direct investment. If the host government pursues appropriate policies, foreign investment can combine capital with local resources and skills, bringing management and labour training, new marketing opportunities and, above all, transfers of technology. But all this is contingent on legal security of investment. As observed earlier, many developing countries have realised as much, setting examples that others will follow. If it were possible to reach agreement on a code of conduct for international investment, taking account of the interests of both potential foreign investors and host countries, this could well promote mutually profitable transfers of resources from developed to developing countries. But international rules would not, by themselves, increase security of investment. In assessing investment risk, firms try to obtain an impression of the prospective host government's overall attitude to, or respect for, law within its own borders. Only changes in attitudes—and a recognition of the real common interest —can attract more foreign direct investment in developing countries.

Important, as these investment concerns are, the paramount common interest is a liberal trading system. Accordingly, the Brandt Commission's recommendation that protectionist measures in developed countries against the exports of developing countries should be rolled back clearly merits the strongest support. Of late, there has been an almost palpable fear among governments of the developed countries that domestic pressures for protection, and the international frictions they generate, will get out of hand.[3] This fear has been borne out, over the last year or so, by one official report after another.[4]

The most important benefit the developed countries can bestow on the developing countries, is the maintenance of stable growth and an open trading system; by comparison with these achievements all the 'concessions' the developed countries may make to the 'demands' of the Group of 77 can do little towards alleviating the plight of poor peoples in the Third World. Once the framework of principles and rules that constitutes the international economic order is reasserted, providing a stable institutional environment, market competition will promote still more rapid economic growth in the Third World. Here is a true common interest. For the framework of principles and rules is equally necessary to developed countries. But it is more than a common interest. It is a recognition of common values.

If an effective international economic system is restored —maintaining the trade rules, maintaining stable monetary conditions and maintaining open markets—the countries which are likely to do best in taking advantage of the opportunities thus created will be those which are most successful in recruiting the talents, the innovation and the resources of private enterprise and in taking advantage of the market mechanism rather than relying on government intervention, control and regulation.

NOTES AND REFERENCES

1.In an analysis published in 1976 by the Brookings Institution in Washington, it was argued: 'Ten years ago, a review of major economic and social problems would have concentrated on asking how government might best deal with them. In today's climate of public opinion, the same review must begin by asking whether government is capable of dealing with them. Ten years ago, government was widely valued as an instrument to resolve problems; today, government itself is widely viewed as the problem.' See Charles Schultz and Henry Owen, *Setting National Priorities: the Next Ten Years* (Washington: Brookings Institution, 1976).

For a recent overview of the problems posed by government intervention in the market process, see Blackhurst, 'The Twilight of Domestic Economic Policies', *The World Economy*, December 1981.

2.At the seventh Economic Summit meeting held in Ottawa in July 1981, the heads of government representing Canada, France, the Federal Republic of Germany, Italy, Japan, the United Kingdom and the United States and the President of the Commission of the European Community made a point, in their conclusions, of reasserting the reliance of policy on the market process. 'We must accept the role of the market in our economies,' their *communiqué* said. 'We must not let transitional measures that may be needed to ease change become permanent forms of protection or subsidy.'

In June 1981, the Bank for International Settlements stated in its *Annual Report* for 1981: 'It is no accident that the growth of government should have gone hand in hand with a long-term worsening in inflation. The commitment to full employment and the emergence of the modern welfare state have changed attitudes and imparted an inflationary bias to economies' (p. 25).

In its *World Economic Outlook* for 1981, the IMF stated: 'At a time when the growth rate of real per capita income was already declining, many governments decided to maintain or even accelerate the expansion of government services and transfers. It is difficult to assess how much the increased tax burden required to finance government activity may have reduced private-sector incentives to work, save and invest in productive capital, but the effect may have been sizeable ... Government intervention in the labour markets, however desirable from a social or political stand-point, has in many cases contributed to inflation and unemployment ... [New] policies should aim at the difficult task of removing barriers that have been erected—sometimes by the authorities themselves—against the free play of market forces in the goods and labor markets' (pp. 8-9).

The July 1981 number of the *OECD Observer* stated: 'Public sector deficits have widened and the size and intrusiveness of the public sector have increased. Many countries consider it imperative to reduce both the weight of government in the economy and the size of its deficit' (p. 13).

In its annual report, *International Trade 1980-81*, the GATT stated: 'If the process of adjustment has gradually become inadequate, it is logical to ask what new obstructions have come about in the last fifteen years. There are many and, in the aggregate, they imply that economic decisions have been increasingly subject not or not only to the criteria of efficiency but also to those of political "acceptability". This tendency has not been just a reflection of the growth of public expenditure relative to GNP—although the two phenomena are related ...

'In a broadly illustrative way, we may distinguish three categories of obstructions which have been, increasingly in recent years, impeding the adjustment process.

'A general feature of the decline in adjustment capacity is the impairment of the pricing mechanism, the function of which is to signal incipient scarcities and redundancies in the system. This is tantamount to saying that the effectiveness of competition has declined. The first category thus includes the most direct obstructions, such as the acceptance—and in some cases enforcement—by public authorities of competition-restricting arrangements among firms, the political determination of particular prices and quantitative import restrictions. Of all the markets in the economy, it is in the labour market and in agriculture that the pricing mechanism has been most impaired. The difficulty of increasing employment by injecting a monetary stimulus into the economy as well as the necessity for various job-creation schemes based on employment subsidies, indicate that the existing unemployment is mainly due to inappropriate *patterns of wages*.

'The second category includes a large variety of measures whose common feature is that they narrow the scope of entrepreneurial initiative and/or create costly delays in the execution of business decisions. This has been perhaps the most rapidly expanding category. Measures in it aim at a variety of objectives, ranging from labour-market to environmental considerations, and differ greatly in form as well as effects between countries.

'Finally, certain aspects of policy practices have significantly attenuated the incentive for firms to adapt and adjust, as various interest groups have become able to influence policy conduct towards the preservation of existing industrial structures. Here we may mention the enforcement of competition laws in such a way that small, less efficient producers are protected against larger and more efficient ones, and the availability of subsidies as well as protection against foreign competition for otherwise unviable enterprises' (Ch. 1).

3.In June 1981, the GATT's Consultative Group of Eighteen, a representative group of high-level officials with responsibilities in the formulation of their countries' trade policies, decided that a special ministerial conference should be convened towards the end of 1982. The *communiqué* issued at the time noted that 'trade relations are beset by a number of complex and potentially disruptive problems, reflecting growing protectionist pressures, and that there is a need for improved international cooperation to solve these problems', adding that 'it would be useful to consider at political level the overall condition of the international trading system'.

4.Apart from the IMF's *World Economic Outlook*, quoted in note 2 above, and the July 1981 number of the *OECD Observer*, see the World Bank's *World Development Report 1981, op. cit.*

Selected Bibliography

SET OUT below is a selected bibliography relating to the issues discussed in this report. It has been confined to books and monographs; articles from journals have been cited in the notes and references. In addition to general titles, there are sections on international institutions, international trade, economic development, policies of developing countries, North-South issues, aid, agriculture and, finally, foreign private investment and the transfer of technology.

General

P. T. BAUER, *Equality, the Third World and Economic Delusion* (London: Weidenfeld & Nicolson, 1981).

JAGDISH N. BHAGWATI and T. N. SRINIVASAN, *International Economic Policy: Theory and Evidence* (Baltimore: Johns Hopkins Press, 1979).

RICHARD BLACKHURST, NICOLAS MARIAN and JAN TUMLIR, *Trade Liberalization, Protectionism and Interdependence*, GATT Studies in International Trade No. 5 (Geneva: GATT Secretariat, 1978).

RICHARD BLACKHURST, NICOLAS MARIAN and JAN TUMLIR, *Adjustment Trade and Growth in Developed and Developing Countries*, GATT Studies in International Trade No. 6 (Geneva: GATT Secretariat, 1978).

Sir Alec Cairncross, Herbert Giersch, Alexander Lamfalussy, Giuseppe Petrilli and Pierre Uri, *Economic Policy for the European Community: the Way Forward* (London: Macmillan, for the Institut für Weltwirtschaft an der Universität Kiel, 1974).

Geoffrey Denton, Seamus O'Cleireacain and Sally Ash, *Trade Effects of Public Subsidies to Private Enterprise* (London: Macmillan, for the Trade Policy Research Centre, 1975; and New York: St Martin's Press, 1975).

Hans-Hinrich Glismann, Hans Rodemer and Frank Wolter, *Zur Natur der Wachstumsschwache in der Bundesrepublik Deutschland: Eine empirische Analyse langer Zyklen wirtschaftlicher Entwicklung*, Kiel Discussion Paper No. 55 (Kiel: Institut für Weltwirtschaft an der Universität Kiel, 1978).

Harry G. Johnson, *Economic Policies Toward Less Developed Countries* (Washington: Brookings Institution, 1967).

Harry G. Johnson, *Technology and Economic Interdependence* (London: Macmillan, for the Trade Policy Research Centre, 1975).

Alasdair I. MacBean and V. N. Balasubramanyam, *Meeting the Third World Challenge*, 2nd ed. (London: Macmillan, for the Trade Policy Research Centre, 1978).

M. M. Postan, *An Economic History of Western Europe* (London: Methuen, 1967).

Kerry Schott, *Industrial Innovation in the United Kingdom, Canada and the United States* (London: Washington and Montreal: British-North American Committee, 1981).

International Institutions

Heinz W. Arndt, *The Economic Lessons of the Nineteen Thirties* (Oxford: Clarendon Press, 1942).

WILLIAM ADAMS BROWN, *The United States and the Restoration of World Trade: an Analysis and Appraisal of the ITO Charter and the General Agreement on Tariffs and Trade* (Washington: Brookings Institution, 1950).

GERARD CURZON, *Multilateral Commercial Diplomacy* (London: Michael Joseph, 1965).

KENNETH W. DAM, *The GATT Law and International Economic Organization* (Chicago and London: University of Chicago Press, 1970).

RICHARD N. GARDNER, *Sterling-Dollar Diplomacy*, 2nd ed. (New York: McGraw-Hill, 1969).

JOHN H. JACKSON, *World Trade and the Law of the GATT* (Indianapolis: Bobbs-Merrill, 1969).

CHARLES P. KINDLEBERGER, *The World Depression 1929-1939* (Harmondsworth: Penguin Books, 1973).

KARIN KOCK, *International Trade Policy and the GATT 1947-1967* (Stockholm: Almqvist & Wiksell, 1969).

EDWARD H. MASON and R. E. ASHER, *The World Bank since Bretton Woods* (Washington: Brookings Institution, 1973).

WILLIAM E. RAPPARD, *Postwar Efforts for Freer Trade* (Geneva: Geneva Research Centre, 1938).

LIONEL ROBBINS, *The Economic Causes of War* (London: Macmillan, 1942).

International Trade

ROBERT E. BALDWIN, *Non-Tariff Distortions of International Trade* (Washington: Brookings Institution 1970).

W. M. CORDEN, *The Theory of Protection* (Oxford: Clarendon Press, 1971).

GERARD CURZON and VICTORIA CURZON, *Hidden Barriers to International Trade*, Thames Essay No. 1 (London: Trade Policy Research Centre, 1970).

HARRY G. JOHNSON, *Comparative Cost and Commercial Policy Theory for a Developing World Economy*, Wiksell Lectures (Stockholm: Almqvist & Wiksell, 1968).

HARRY G. JOHNSON (ed.), *Trade Strategy for Rich and Poor Nations* (London: Allen & Unwin, for the Trade Policy Research Centre, 1971; and Toronto: University of Toronto Press, 1972).

ALBERT O. HIRSCHMAN, *National Power and the Structure of Foreign Trade* (Berkeley and Los Angeles: University of California Press, 1945).

ROBERT E. HUDEC, *Adjudication of International Trade Disputes*, Thames Essay No. 16 (London: Trade Policy Research Centre, 1978).

DONALD B. KEESING and MARTIN WOLF, *Textile Quotas against Developing Countries*, Thames Essay No. 23 (London: Trade Policy Research Centre, 1980).

MELVYN KRAUSS, *The New Protectionism* (Oxford: Basil Blackwell, 1979).

HAL B. LARY, *Imports of Manufactures from Less Developed Countries* (London and New York: Columbia University Press, 1968).

I. M. D. LITTLE, TIBOR SCITOVSKY and M. FG. SCOTT, *Industry and Trade in Some Developing Countries: a Comparative Study* (London: Oxford University Press, for the OECD, 1971).

HARALD B. MALMGREN, *International Order for Public Subsidies*, Thames Essay No. 11 (London: Trade Policy Research Centre, 1977).

BAHRAM NOWZAD, *The Rise in Protectionism* (Washington: IMF, 1978).

DAVID ROBERTSON, *Fail Safe Systems for Trade Liberalisation*, Thames Essay No. 12 (London: Trade Policy Research Centre, 1977).

M. FG. SCOTT, W. M. CORDEN and I. M. D. LITTLE, *The Case against General Import Restrictions*, Thames Essay No. 24 (London: Trade Policy Research Centre, 1980).

SECRETARY GENERAL OF THE OECD, *The Impact of the Newly Industrialising Countries* (Paris: OECD Secretariat, 1979).

Economic Development

JAGDISH BHAGWATI, *The Economics of Underdeveloped Countries* (London: Weidenfeld & Nicolson, 1966).

P. T. BAUER and BASIL YAMEY, *The Economics of Under-developed Countries* (Cambridge: Cambridge University Handbooks, 1957).

JUERGEN B. DONGES and LOTTE MÜLLER-OHLSEN, *Aussenwirtschaftsstrategien und Industrialisierung in Entwicklungslanden* (Tübingen: J. C. B. Mohr, for the Institut für Weltwirtschaft an der Universität Kiel, 1978).

HELEN HUGHES (ed.), *Prospects for Partnership* (Baltimore: Johns Hopkins Press, for the World Bank, 1973).

SIMON KUZNETS, *Economic Growth of Nations* (Cambridge, Mass.: Harvard University Press, 1971).

Sir ARTHUR LEWIS, *Theory of Economic Growth* (London: Allen & Unwin, 1955).

ALASDAIR I. MACBEAN, *Export Instability and Economic Development* (London: Allen & Unwin, 1966).

GERALD M. MEIER, *The International Economics of Development: Theory and Policy* (London: Harper & Row, 1968).

GERALD M. MEIER, *Leading Issues in Development Economics* (London: Oxford University Press, 1970).

J. W. Mellor, *The New Economics of Growth* (Ithaca: Cornell University Press, 1976).

A. K. Sen, *Employment, Technology and Development* (London: Oxford University Press, 1971).

Policies for Development

Shankar N. Acharya and Bruce Johnston (eds), *Two Studies of Development in Sub-Saharan Africa*, World Bank Staff Working Paper No. 300 (Washington: World Bank, 1978).

Bela Balassa and Associates, *The Structure of Protection in Developing Countries* (Baltimore: Johns Hopkins Press, for the World Bank, 1971).

Bela Balassa, *Policy Reform in Developing Countries* (Oxford: Pergamon Press, 1977).

Jagdish Bhagwati and Padma Desai, *India: Planning for Industrialisation—Industrialisation and Trade Policies since 1981* (London, New York and Bombay: Oxford University Press, for the OECD, 1970).

Jagdish N. Bhagwati, *Foreign Trade Regimes and Economic Development: Anatomy and Consequences of Exchange Control Regimes* (Cambridge, Mass.: Ballinger, for the National Bureau of Economic Research, 1979).

John Cody, Helen Hughes and David Wall (eds), *Policies for Industrial Progress in Developing Countries* (Oxford and New York: Oxford University Press, for the World Bank, 1980).

Walter Galenson (ed.), *Economic Growth and Structural Change in Taiwan: the Postwar Experience of the Republic of China* (Ithaca: Cornell University Press, 1979).

Anne O. Krueger, *Foreign Trade Regimes and Economic Development: Liberalization Attempts and Consequences* (Cambridge, Mass.: Ballinger, for the National Bureau of Economic Research, 1978).

FRANK KIM and LARRY E. WESTPHAL, *Foreign Trade Regimes and Economic Development: South Korea* (New York and London: Columbia University Press, for the National Bureau of Economic Research, 1975).

ANGUS MADDISON, *Class Structure and Economic Growth: India and Pakistan Since the Moghuls* (London: Allen & Unwin, 1971).

BERND STECHER, *Erfolgsbedingungen der Importsubstitution und der Exportdiversifizierung im Industrialisierungsprozess: Die Erfahrungen in Chile, Mexiko und SüdKorea*, Kieler Studien No. 136 (Tübingen: J. C. B. Mohr, for the Institut für Weltwirtschaft an der Universität Kiel, 1976).

LANCE TAYLOR, EDMAR L. BACHA, ELIANA A. CARDOSO and FRANK J. LYSY, *Models of Growth and Distribution for Brazil* (New York: Oxford University Press, for the World Bank, 1980).

WILLIAM G. TYLER, *Manufactured Export Expansion and Industrialization in Brazil*, Kieler Studien No. 134 (Tübingen: J. C. B. Mohr, for the Institut für Weltwirtschaft an der Universität Kiel, 1976).

North-South Dialogue

JAGDISH BHAGWATI (ed.), *The New International Economic Order: the North-South Debate* (Cambridge, Mass.: MIT Press, 1977).

W. M. CORDEN, *The NIEO: a Cool Look*, Thames Essay No. 21 (London: Trade Policy Research Centre, 1979).

ISAIAH FRANK, *The 'Graduation' Issue in Trade Policy Towards LDCs*, World Bank Staff Working Paper No. 334 (Washington: World Bank, 1979).

HERBERT GIERSCH (ed.), *Reshaping the World Economic Order* (Tübingen: J. C. B. Mohr, for the Institut für Weltwirtschaft an der Universität Kiel, 1977).

INDEPENDENT COMMISSION ON INTERNATIONAL DEVELOP-
MENT ISSUES, *North-South: a Programme for Survival*
(London and Sydney: Pan Books, 1980).

TRACY MURRAY, *Trade Preferences for Developing Countries*
(London: Macmillan, 1977).

HANS SINGER and JAVED ANSARI, *Rich and Poor Nations*
(London: Allen & Unwin, 1977).

Aid

P. T. BAUER, *Dissent on Development* (London: Weidenfeld
& Nicolson, 1971).

JAGDISH BHAGWATI and RICHARD S. ECKAUS, *Foreign Aid*
(Harmondsworth: Penguin Books, 1970).

COMMISSION ON INTERNATIONAL DEVELOPMENT, *Partners in
Development*, Pearson Report (New York: Praeger, for
the World Bank, 1969).

GERALD HOLTHAM and ARTHUR HAZELWOOD, *Aid and
Inequality in Kenya* (London: Croom Helm, for the Overseas Development Institute, 1976).

NEIL HERMAN JACOBY, *US Aid to Taiwan: a Study of
Foreign Aid, Self-help and Development* (New York:
Praeger, 1966).

DEEPAK LAL, *Poverty, Power and Prejudice: the North-South
Confrontation* (London: Fabian Society, 1978).

I. M. D. LITTLE and J. M. CLIFFORD, *International Aid*
(London: Allen & Unwin, 1965).

RAYMOND F. MIKESELL, *The Economics of Foreign Aid*
(London: Weidenfeld & Nicolson, 1968).

KATHRYN MORTON, *Aid and Dependence: British Aid to
Malawi* (London: Croom Helm, for the Overseas
Development Institute, 1975).

GÖRAN OHLIN, *Foreign Aid Policies Reconsidered* (Paris: Development Centre of the OECD, 1966).

Agriculture

D. GALE JOHNSON, *World Agriculture in Disarray* (London: Macmillan, for the Trade Policy Research Centre, 1973; and New York: St Martin's Press, 1973).

JOHN W. MELLOR, *The Economics of Agricultural Development* (Ithaca: Cornell University Press, 1966).

THEODORE W. SCHULTZ, *Transforming Traditional Agriculture* (New Haven: Yale University Press, 1964).

Foreign Private Investment

V. N. BALASUBRAMANYAM, *Multinational Enterprises and the Third World*, Thames Essay No. 26 (London: Trade Policy Research Centre, 1980).

PETER DRYSDALE (ed.), *Direct Foreign Investment in Asia and the Pacific* (Canberra: Australian National University Press, 1972; and Toronto: University of Toronto Press, 1972).

JOHN H. DUNNING (ed.), *The Multinational Enterprise* (London: Allen & Unwin, 1971).

JOHN H. DUNNING (ed.), *International Investment* (Harmondsworth: Penguin Books, 1972).

CHARLES KINDLEBERGER, *American Business Abroad: Six Lectures on Direct Investment* (New Haven: Yale University Press, 1969).

HLA MYINT, *South East Asia's Economy: Development Policies in the 1970s* (Harmondsworth: Penguin Books, 1973).

GRANT L. REUBER *et al.*, *Private Foreign Investment in Development* (London: Oxford University Press, for the Development Centre, OECD, 1973).

RAYMOND VERNON, *Sovereignty at Bay* (New York: Basic Books, 1971).

List of Thames Essays

OCCASIONAL papers of the Trade Policy Research Centre are published under the omnibus heading of Thames Essays. Set out below are the particulars of those published to date. The first twenty-two titles were published in an octavo-size format.

1   GERARD and VICTORIA CURZON, *Hidden Barriers to International Trade* (1970), 70 pp., £1.50.

2   T. E. JOSLING, *Agriculture and Britain's Trade Policy Dilemma* (1970), 43 pp., £1.00.

3   GERARD and VICTORIA CURZON, *Global Assault on Non-tariff Trade Barriers* (1972), 40 pp., £1.50.

4   BRIAN HINDLEY, *Britain's Position on Non-tariff Protection* (1972), 64 pp., £1.50.

5   GEOFFREY DENTON and SEAMUS O'CLEIREACAIN, *Subsidy Issues in International Commerce* (1972), 64 pp., £1.50.

6   GEORGE F. RAY, *Western Europe and the Energy Crisis* (1975), 65 pp., £2.00.

7   THEODORE GEIGER, JOHN VOLPE and ERNEST H. PREEG, *North American Integration and Economic Blocs* (1975), 62 pp., £2.00.

8   HUGH CORBET, W. M. CORDEN, BRIAN HINDLEY, ROY BATCHELOR and PATRICK MINFORD, *On How to Cope with Britain's Trade Position* (1977), 80 pp., £2.00.

9 PETER LLOYD, *Anti-dumping Actions and the GATT System* (1977), 58 pp., £2.00.

10 T. E. JOSLING, *Agriculture in the Tokyo Round Negotiations* (1977), 48 pp., £2.00.

11 HARALD B. MALMGREN, *International Order for Public Subsidies* (1977), 74 pp., £2.00.

12 DAVID ROBERTSON, *Fail Safe Systems for Trade Liberalisation* (1977), 68 pp., £2.00.

13 SIDNEY GOLT, *Developing Countries in the GATT System* (1978), 40 pp., £2.90.

14 THEODOR HEIDHUES, T. E. JOSLING, CHRISTOPHER RITSON and STEFAN TANGERMANN, *Common Prices and Europe's Farm Policy* (1978), 84 pp., £2.00.

15 HANS BÖHME, *Restraints on Competition in World Shipping* (1978), 80 pp., £3.00.

16 ROBERT E. HUDEC, *Adjudication of International Trade Disputes* (1978), 92 pp., £3.00.

17 STUART HARRIS, MARK SALMON and BEN SMITH, *Analysis of Commodity Markets for Policy Purposes* (1978), 82 pp., £3.00.

18 ROBERT Z. ALIBER, *Stabilising World Monetary Arrangements* (1979), 50 pp., £3.00.

19 ROBERT L. CARTER and GERARD M. DICKINSON, *Barriers to Trade in Insurance* (1979), 72 pp., £3.00.

20 GEOFFREY SMITH, *Westminster Reform: Learning from Congress* (1979), 54 pp., £2.00.

21 W. M. CORDEN, *The NIEO Proposals: a Cool Look* (1979), 58 pp., £3.00.

22 ROBERT E. BALDWIN, *Beyond the Tokyo Round Negotiations* (1979), 64 pp., £3.00.

23 DONALD B. KEESING and MARTIN WOLF, *Textile Quotas against Developing Countries* (1980), 224 pp., £6.00.

24 M. FG. SCOTT, W. M. CORDEN and I. M. D. LITTLE, *The Case against General Import Restrictions* (1980), 105 pp., £5.00.

25 VICTORIA CURZON PRICE, *Unemployment and Other Non-work Issues* (1980), 61 pp., £3.00.

26 V. N. BALASUBRAMANYAM, *Multinational Enterprises and the Third World* (1980), 87 pp., £3.00.

27 T. E. JOSLING, MARK LANGWORTHY and SCOTT PEARSON, *Options for Farm Policy in the European Community* (1981), 94 pp., £3.00.

28 DEEPAK LAL, *Resurrection of the Pauper-labour Argument* (1981), 82pp., £2.00.

29 ISAIAH FRANK, *Trade Policy Issues of Interest to the Third World* (1981), 78pp., £2.00.

PUBLICATIONS of the Trade Policy Research Centre can best be obtained, with a significant saving both financially and in terms of time and trouble, by becoming a member.

Membership of the Centre is open to individuals, firms and other institutions involved or interested in international business and economic affairs. Applications for membership have to be approved by the Council.

Annual subscriptions, corresponding to the calendar year, break down into (a) individual — or personal — members, (b) library subscribers and (c) corporate members who divide into commercial and non-commercial institutions. The subscription for individuals is £35 (or its equivalent in other currencies at the time of payment), while that for library subscribers is £40. Subscriptions for corporate members are by arrangement, there being a guide to the level of them which may be obtained on application, but the minimum level for non-commercial institutions is £100.

What are the benefits of membership? The work of the Centre is set out in a brochure which includes a list of publications. But, in brief, members

• are kept abreast of the complex issues of international economic relations that affect the environment in which businesses and governments have to operate;

• are sent *The World Economy*, the Centre's quarterly journal;

• are sent Thames Essays as they are published;

• are able to purchase at a 25 per cent discount major volumes published for the Centre by commercial publishers;

• are circulated other papers, articles and so on that are considered worthy of particular attention; and

• are notified of all the Centre's dinners, lectures and other meetings, which provide an opportunity for members to meet others actively interested in international business and economic affairs — this last mainly being of value to individual members or corporate members located themselves, or having representatives located, in London or its vicinity.

Since the Centre's publications are not meant to be produced, and its activities are not meant to be conducted, on a regular basis, subscriptions paid during the year are not adjusted on a *pro rata* basis. Each subscription covers all the publications produced during the year in question.

Enquiries about membership, subscriptions and publications should be addressed to the Director, Trade Policy Research Centre, 1 Gough Square, London EC4A 3DE, United Kingdom (Telephone: 01-353 6371).